Presenting Arms

Presenting Arms: Museum Representation of British Military History, 1660–1900

Peter Thwaites

Leicester University Press
London and New York

LEICESTER UNIVERSITY PRESS
A Cassell Imprint
Wellington House, 125 Strand, London WC2R 0BB
215 Park Avenue South, New York, NY 10003, USA

First published in 1996

British Library Cataloguing-in-Publication Data
A catalogue record for this book is available from The British Library

ISBN 0-7185-1534-X

Library of Congress Cataloging-in-Publication Data
Thwaites, Peter, 1944–
    Presenting arms : museum representation of British military
history, 1660–1900 / Peter Thwaites.
      p. cm.—(Leicester museum studies)
    Includes bibliographical references and index.
    ISBN 0–7185–1534–X
    1. Military museums—Great Britain—History. 2. Great Britain—
History, Military—Sources. I. Title. II. Series : Leicester
museum studies series.
    U13.G7T48 1996
    355′.00941′075—dc20   95–31844
                                                         CIP

Typeset by Keystroke, Jacaranda Lodge, Wolverhampton
Printed and bound in Great Britain by Biddles Limited, Guildford and King's Lynn

For Stephanie, Simon and Jane

Contents

General Preface to Series

Museums are an international growth area. The number of museums in the world is now very large, embracing some 13,500 in Europe, of which 2,300 are in the United Kingdom: some 7,000 in North America; 2,800 in Australasia and Asia; and perhaps 2,000 in the rest of the world. The range of museum orientation is correspondingly varied and covers all aspects of the natural and the human heritage. Paralleling the growth in numbers comes a major development in the opportunities open to museums to play an important part in shaping cultural perceptions within their communities, as people everywhere become more aware of themselves and their surroundings.

Accordingly, museums are now reviewing and rethinking their role as the storehouses of knowledge and as the presenters to people of their relationship to their own environment and past and to those of others. Traditional concepts of what a museum is, and how it should operate, are confronted by contemporary intellectual, social and political concerns which deal with questions like the validity of value judgements, bias in collecting and display, the de-mystifying of specialized knowledge, the protection of the environment, and the nature of our place in history.

These are all large and important areas and the debate is an international one. The series *Leicester Museum Studies* is designed to make a significant contribution to the development of new theory and practice across the broad range of the museum operation. Individual volumes in the series will consider in depth particular museums areas, defined either by disciplinary field or by function. Many strands of opinion will be represented, but the series as a whole will present a body of discussion and ideas which should help to redress both the present poverty of theory and the absence of a reference collection of substantial published material, which curators everywhere currently see as a fundamental lack. The community, quite rightly, is now asking more of its museums. More must be given, and to achieve this, new directions and new perspectives must be generated. In this project, *Leicester Museum Studies* is designed to play its part.

SUSAN M. PEARCE
Department of Museum Studies
University of Leicester

List of Illustrations

Abbreviations

AGAI	Army General and Administrative Instructions
AIM	Association of Independent Museums
AMOT	Army Museums Ogilby Trust
ARP	Air Raid Precaution
DNH	Department of National Heritage
IRA	Irish Republican Army
IWM	Imperial War Museum
MGC	Museums and Galleries Commission
MoD	Ministry of Defence
NAM	National Army Museum
POW	Prisoner of War
RAF	Royal Air Force
REME	Royal Electrical and Mechanical Engineers
RHQ	Regimental Head Quarters
RUSI	Royal United Service Institution
SHCG	Social History Curators Group
TA	Territorial Army
VC	Victoria Cross
WHAM	Women, Heritage and Museums

Appendix

Introduction

Museums of the armed services represent a long and fine tradition. They are part of the culture of these services. Yet they are also part of a wider national and international culture of scholarship and communication of knowledge.
(Museums and Galleries Commission 1990:44)

Military museums are not, as a category, celebrated for originality of conception, style, first-class showmanship or for humanity.
(Judge, European Museum of the Year, 1983)

The British armed forces have a long and glorious tradition. The Royal Navy has been in existence for 450 years, and for over 100 years it was the most powerful and formidable navy in the world. The British Army is younger, but some regiments have a continuous history of more than 300 years, and it has acquired a well-deserved reputation for its skill and courage. The Royal Air Force, although less than 100 years old, has already demonstrated, during the military conflicts of this century, bravery and technical expertise second to none. The British pride themselves on not being a warlike people, but their armed forces have helped to establish Britain in the forefront of nations and to create the largest empire the world has seen, as well as keeping the country free from invasion for 300 years. This military success has helped, as much as industrial and economic achievements, to mould the British nation.

In Britain many statues, public buildings and squares commemorate these military achievements. That is quite normal in many countries. What is more unusual is the large number of military museums this country boasts.

In 1989 a working party of the Museums and Galleries Commission, led by Admiral Sir David Williams CGB DL, carried out a survey into Britain's military museums (MGC 1990). This revealed that there are over 200 museums in Britain dealing with some aspect of military history or containing military collections. Of these, five national museums, four museums designated under the 1983 Heritage Act and approximately 160 regimental and corps museums are devoted solely to this subject. Together they constitute probably the largest group of specialist museums in the country. Yet they often seem less highly regarded within the museum world than other specialist museums.

There are, I suspect, a number of reasons for this attitude. In the first place, as Stephen Wood, the Director of the Scottish United Services Museum, suggests (Wood 1987a), some museum professionals seem embarrassed by military collections. These collections, after all,

1

represent and are often accused of glorifying militarism and imperial-
ism, two aspects of our history which many find repugnant. Others
argue, as we shall see, that, while military collections are important, the
way they are interpreted in military museums is almost wholly irrelevant
to the modern world (Hudson 1991:17).

Secondly, military museums may be considered beyond the pale
because of the unprofessional image of their staff and the poor quality
of some of their displays. Stephen Wood (1986b:20) has identified
a common picture of the regimental museum curator. 'He, and it is
invariably the male of the species,' says Wood,

will be thought of as a retired serviceman, probably an officer, given to wearing
clothes that are as unfashionable as possible . . . and to having neatly cut hair and
polished shoes. He will exude an air of amateur scholarship tinged with whiffs of
damp dogs, pipe tobacco and properly hung pheasant. The image of the grouse
moor will combine with that of the Established Church and that of the politically
conservative to round off the caricature.

He will also, though this is not mentioned by Stephen Wood, be
untrained as a curator (except for a short course at the National Army
Museum[1]) and will never have attended a Museums Association Annual
Conference or a Social History Curators Group Meeting.

Regimental museum curators are, moreover, often part-timers who
have to carry out their curatorial duties while acting as a Regimental
Secretary or holding down some other regimental or military post,
while the relatively few full-time regimental museum curators often
have very limited facilities and resources with which to carry out their
tasks. This largely explains the poor standard of display and the
appalling examples of curatorial and conservational neglect that can be
seen in some military museums, and which gives them a bad name
amongst civilian museum curators (Wood 1986a:13 and MGC 1990:38).

However, many military museums do achieve a relatively high
standard of display and look after their artifacts well, which is wholly
attributable to the dedication and enthusiasm of their curators (MGC
1990:28). In any case, even if in the past military curators tended
to see themselves as a group apart, more interested in preserving the
spirit and history of their regiment than in the niceties of curatorial
practice, they are now aware of the standards they need to attain and are
increasingly seeking help and advice from the Army Museums Ogilby
Trust (AMOT), the national military museums, the Area Museums
Councils, or their local museum service. Moreover, the accusation of
unprofessionalism could not be levelled at the staff of the national
museums, nor at local authority curators of military collections, nor at
the increasing number of museum professionals who are taking charge
of regimental museums.

Perhaps a more serious accusation that has been levelled at military
museums, and more particularly at regimental and corps museums,
is that they are, as Stephen Wood (1986b:20) has said, not like other
mainstream museums but instead are 'family' museums (the family

being the regiment or corps); they represent primarily the interests of their particular family while virtually ignoring the general public. W. C. Lazenby (1989:22–3), in an unpublished thesis, adds that 'Regimental museums are little more than extensions of a very specialized form of written military history – the regimental history . . . ' the purpose of which 'is to sustain morale and teach recruits the behaviour which is expected of them in combat, by giving them a past to which they must prove themselves worthy'. Undoubtedly, regimental museums have tended to concentrate on highlighting the achievements of their own regiment while ignoring the broader context of events (MGC 1990:39). Moreover, in the past (and even to some extent today), their displays, and those of some of the national military museums, have been aimed purely at enthusiasts or members of the regiment (MGC 1990:39), and have concentrated on the esoteric and particular rather than on a general narrative.

These failings could partly be blamed on their curators, but they are also the fault of their governing bodies. As will become clear, it is claimed that the Ministry of Defence (MoD), the overall manager and paymaster of nearly half of these museums, has not had a consistent policy towards its museums, and has not, until recently, provided any guidelines on what the museums' aims and objectives should be. It recognizes, though, that they perform valuable public relations and training tasks for the armed services, and it in turn provides some financial support for approximately 100 military museums.

Most of these museums also receive considerable financial and practical support from their regiments or regimental old comrades association. Indeed, the day-to-day management of the museum is in the hands of trustees drawn from their ranks. But trustees are usually serving or retired members of the regiment who have no museum training or any involvement in the more general museum scene. Their primary interest is the preservation of the history and traditions of their regiment; and often, it appears, they are only concerned with the way in which this history is presented to the other members and ex-members of the regiment who visit the museum. It is at this level that Stephen Wood's charge that these are primarily 'family' museums seems most true. Yet even here things are changing. The tireless work of both AMOT, the national military museums and the Area Museum Councils has helped to broaden the outlook of these trustees, and the exigencies of the current economic environment are forcing them to try to find ways to increase the appeal of their museums to the general public. The new Museums and Galleries Commission Registration Scheme, which links eligibility for grant aid to the achievement of certain standards in record keeping, conservation and management of the collections, has also encouraged these trustees to take a more professional stance on the running of their museums.

These military museums are changing, therefore, and they are gradually throwing off their old-fashioned, unprofessional and elitist image. As a result they seem to be overcoming some of the prejudice which may have existed against them in the past within the museum profession; military museums and their collections were discussed, for example, at the Museums Association Annual Conference in 1990, and in both the February 1987 and November 1991 editions of the *Museums Journal.*

Moreover, the general public seems to have an unfailing interest in these types of collections, despite the poor way they have often been displayed in the past. Military museums receive approximately five million visitors a year, and while many of these will be ex-servicemen and their relations, not all of them can be members of the 'family'. There are, I think, three main reasons for this enthusiasm for military museums shown by the general public. In the first place, personal memories of the major wars of this century are still strong, or are part of the folk memory of those who did not endure them. This is reinforced by the undying interest in these conflicts shown by film-makers, television producers and book publishers. Military museums provide, therefore, a place where people can have contact with real objects from their own past or from their fantasies. Secondly, again perhaps against our wishes, military objects can exert a fascination greater than a plough or a milk churn. From the bloodstained coat or bayonet to complex instruments of war like tanks, aeroplanes or submarines, these objects can be exciting, 'sexy', and curiously familiar. Moreover, they can arouse the interest of collectors or enthusiasts who visit military museums to see rare types or perfect specimens, in the same way that butterfly collectors may visit natural history museums or fossil hunters seek out geological collections.

Finally, military history may be a more approachable subject for a large number of people than more esoteric disciplines like geology, natural history or fine art. Most little boys seem to play at soldiers, while many adults, both male and female, still enjoy military parades and military bands. Moreover, physical courage and endurance, which are the lifeblood of military history and military museum collections, are still highly rated virtues which can be experienced vicariously during a visit to a military museum.

There is, then, an apparent paradox of a large group of museums enjoying a substantial number of visitors each year, which often fails to receive the kind of attention it deserves. One of the main aims of this book, therefore, is to shed more light on the origins, purpose and objectives of these museums, so that museum professionals and other people interested in museology will better understand the reasons for the way in which they have grown and developed, and the constraints, both past and present, under which they operate and which affect the way they present the story they have to tell. I also intend to show and discuss how these museums attempt to display different aspects of military history, and how, at present, these displays are being affected by the need to find a new audience and a new role in the face of the changes which are taking place in the military, political and social environments of this country.

The book will concentrate on museum provision for 1660 to 1900. This time-scale has been chosen because it covers the period from the formation of some of the original units of the first British professional standing army and the parallel emergence of the Royal Navy as a permanent, professional force to the beginnings of the citizen armies of the twentieth century. During these years men normally signed on for life, which meant that they generally served for at least 25 years in the same army unit, though sailors probably had several ships during their service. In both cases, they were operating within organizations with their own laws, customs, traditions, language, loyalties and specialist trades which separated the men from their civilian contemporaries. Military bodies became virtually closed societies. Moreover, more than half of those in the army and the majority of sailors served far away from these shores and lived lives beyond the comprehension of the average British subject, which only helped to increase the separateness of service life from that led by civilians. It is true that many civilians gained some military experience by serving part-time in this country in the militia or volunteer forces, but they had comparatively little in common with the regular troops. Though their lives were very different, their place in the story will be considered in Chapter 7.

In contrast the period since 1900 has been dominated by the citizen armies of the two world wars and the national service forces of the post Second World War era. The line between serviceman and civilian has become blurred, particularly as the experiences of the civilians on the home front in wartime have been, in many ways, just as important to the military history of this century as those of the fighting man and woman engaged overseas. This is, of course, an equally valid period to examine, and some museums, including the Imperial War Museum, are devoted to this study. But I have limited my work to the earlier period, when the social and military histories of the armed forces can, to some extent, be examined in a museum context as separate entities.

Another factor affecting the choice of the period for this study is the dramatic change in the nature of twentieth-century warfare. Up to the end of the nineteenth century, warfare had changed comparatively little in a thousand years, and still depended largely on the strength, determination and courage of the individual soldier or sailor. The most technically advanced pieces of equipment in use were the warship and the artillery piece, both of which had evolved slowly over several hundred years. Since the latter half of the nineteenth century, and particularly since 1900, however, both warfare and the work of the soldier and sailor have been dramatically altered by the invention of, amongst other things, the machine gun, the motor car, the tank, the submarine, the aeroplane, radio, radar, the ballistic missile, chemical warfare and the atomic bomb. The military museums which set out to record the use of these inventions – the Tank Museum, the Royal Navy Submarine Museum, the RAF Museum, the Museum of Army Transport, the REME Museum and the Royal Signals Museum, amongst others – are, therefore, museums of technology as well as military museums, and have a complex story to tell which goes far beyond merely displaying the history and achievements of their unit, or recounting the social history of their members. I decided, therefore, that this study should focus on the museum provision which concentrates on the exploits of flesh and bone, and that I would not complicate the story by examining, as well, the impact on military history displays of the technological developments of the twentieth century. Hopefully other studies, covering this later period, will be produced in the future.

Much of this work may also seem to focus on army museums (particularly as, for the sake of simplicity, I use the term 'military' throughout to encompass both the navy and the army). This is purely because there are only two naval museums covering this period, the Royal Naval Museum and the Royal Marines Museum, augmented by part of the collection of the National Maritime Museum and the Scottish United Services Museum (whose naval gallery is closed at present), together with a small number of historic ships, from which to draw examples. There are, on the other hand, over 150 regimental and corps museums, in addition to the National Army Museum and the military galleries of the Scottish United Services Museum, containing displays on the British Army.

It is perhaps useful to try to explain at this point some of the main reasons behind the considerable difference in museum provision between the two services. Life in the Royal Navy centres, of course, on its ships. Men served for months or sometimes years in these vessels and had no land base they could call home. Royal Navy ships before the twentieth century were also not noted for the spaciousness of their crews' quarters; even the officers' cabins were often just small sections of the deck walled off by canvas. It was not possible, therefore, for ordinary sailors, or for their officers, to accumulate many souvenirs or trophies during their service. Indeed, at least one eighteenth-century senior officer, Admiral Edward Boscawen, was determined that his officers should not have more permanent quarters, 'since this only pandered to their acquisitive instincts and hampered the clearing of the ship for action' (Turner 1956:89). Moreover, naval ships were decommissioned every few years to be either scrapped or refurbished. This meant that it was unlikely that trophies acquired by the ship's crew would stay on board for many years, and end up in time in a museum.

Some interesting and historically significant artifacts survived, of course, carried home in the sailor's trunk, or, like ships' bells and figureheads, preserved when the ship was scrapped. Indeed, two of this country's most important historical military artifacts are ships: one, the *Mary Rose*, dug up from the sea bottom and providing a unique insight into the naval and social life of the sixteenth century, and the other, HMS *Victory*, Nelson's flagship and the symbol of the British navy in the Napoleonic period. But, given the exigencies of naval service and the fate of its ships, it is not surprising that separate museums do not exist for all its vessels.

The British Army, on the other hand, existed from 1660 until the twentieth century as a set of largely stable units, often stationed in the same place for a number of years or with a set depot in which historic artifacts could accumulate. As we shall see, the officers' messes provided a natural home for such objects and, from the end of the eighteenth century onwards, the common soldier lived in a barracks which allowed him slightly more space than sailors had in which to store personal belongings and souvenirs. These two sources were eventually to provide the core of the historical collections of the many regimental museums.

Another largely accidental cause of the survival of so many regimental museums and, incidentally, the reason why this country has so many more military museums than any other nation, is the county connection which our regiments enjoy (Hudson 1991:17). At the beginning of the period of this study, regiments were raised and led, in an echo of the feudal arrangement, by wealthy individuals who gave their names to the regiments. This system continued for 100 years but was eventually scrapped, partly because it caused some confusion, as units changed their name with each new commander, but, more importantly, because the power given to individuals to raise units in return for payment from the Crown led to corruption and misappropriation.

King George II introduced the numbering of units in order of precedence[2], for example the 21st Foot, or the 14th Hussars, and his successor, King George III, insisted that the infantry regiments should adopt a county name and cultivate a connection with that county which might be useful for recruiting. Some of these county connections were never very strong, however, and, as regiments tended to recruit from wherever their Depot Companies happened to be, rather than in their designated county, by the 1870s the original county association had often changed or was no longer valid or important[3]. But a re-organization of the army, introduced in 1881, dropped the numbering of infantry units while retaining and rationalizing the county connec-tions. Thus, for example, the 17th (Leicestershire) Regiment of Foot became the Leicestershire Regiment, and the 12th (East Suffolk) Regiment of Foot became the Suffolk Regiment. Cavalry units did not receive this local nomenclature, but their equivalent in the volunteer forces, the yeomanry units, had always been county based, and bore county names in their titles.

This local connection has meant that in many cases, when regimental museums have been in danger of closing, the local museum service has been willing to take over the collection, or even in some cases the whole museum, of a regiment which bears its county's name and in which many local people would have served. In any case, it is possible that this particular way of naming regiments may have given them an apparent and lasting individuality which a numbering system would not encourage, and thereby assisted the survival of the many stories and traditions, as well as the feeling of unit pride, which provides the backbone of their museums.

I was aware when I began this study that I would have to introduce some military history to set the context within which I could examine museum provision in certain areas. While I have tried not to turn this book into a pocket military history of the period, I hope that I have supplied enough information and explanation to avoid the kind of obscurity for which military museums are often themselves castigated.

This study begins, where arguably all studies of museums should, with an examination of the nature and origins of their collections and a brief history of the formation and purposes of these museums. In subsequent chapters I shall discuss the way in which military history in all its forms has been, is being, and may in the future be recorded and displayed in British military museums and in other museums with substantial military collections.

It has not been possible for me to visit all the military museums in this country, though I have tried to see a large and, I hope, representative sample. Nor is it feasible in a book of this size to draw on all the possible examples of relevant displays or artifacts that I have seen in the course of my research. The failure to mention a particular museum or a particular display does not imply a criticism of them, nor does it suggest that I do not think them worthy of inclusion here.

This project began at the suggestion of Professor Susan Pearce, and I am grateful to her for entrusting it to my hands, and for all her subsequent help and advice. I have also received encouragement from her colleague, Gaynor Kavanagh, who was kind enough to read and comment on a draft of one of the chapters. Colonel Peter Walton, former Secretary of the Army Museums Ogilby Trust, read a complete draft of the book and pointed out a number of factual and historical errors, though he cannot be blamed, of course, for any others that have slipped through. I am very grateful to him for giving up so much of his spare time to help me in this way. Dr Peter Boyden, Head of the Archives, Photographs, Film and Sound Department of the National Army Museum, also read a draft chapter of my book and made a number of valuable comments, as well as opening up some new lines of enquiry for me.

I should like to thank Andrew Gladwell, Assistant Curator of the Royal Engineers Museum, for sending me some very useful material on the history of his museum, and for his subsequent help with photographs. I am also grateful to Gareth Gill, Curator of the 1st The Queen's Dragoon Guards Regimental Museum, and to the many other curators of military collections and museums who were kind enough to answer my questions or supply me with photographs. I should like to acknowledge the kindness of the trustees of those museums which gave me permission to publish photographs from their collections, and to thank Bryan Carpenter of Town and Country Photographers who copied the photographs for me and produced the prints used in this book.

No study of this kind could proceed without access to printed sources, and I should like to thank the Librarian and staff of the University of Leicester Library, the staff of the Library and Archives of the National Army Museum and Jay Heywood of the Department of Arts Policy and Management of City University for all their assistance with my research.

I must mention the considerable help I have received from my friend, Philip Reed, Curator of the Cabinet War Rooms, who, in addition to the encouragement he has always given me, managed to persuade his wife, Sally Blaxland, that she would enjoy the unenviable task of reading my draft and commenting on my prose style! She helped me to remove the worst excesses, but cannot be held responsible for the errors and obscurities that remain. I am most grateful to her.

I have enjoyed the moral support of my colleagues in the Royal Signals Museum, and the special help of Jan Nicholson, who prepared the final typescript. I should also like to thank John MacDonald, the Curator of the Auchindrain Museum of Country Life, whose friendship sustained me during my museum studies, and with whom I have had many useful and enlightening discussions on museological and practical issues.

But my greatest debt is to my family. I have always received great encouragement from my brother, David Thwaites, and my sister, Margaret Roberts, but it is Stephanie, Simon and Jane who have given me the most practical and moral support and have suffered the most inconvenience during the two-and-a-half years it has taken to write this book. To my wife and children I dedicate this work. I hope they will think it was all worthwhile.

Notes

1. It could be argued that, after their National Army Museum course, these military museum curators are better trained than many members of the staff of the small independent museums.
2. This was usually based on the date of foundation of the regiment.
3. In 1782, for example, the 14th Regiment of Foot adopted the title 'Bedfordshire' because it recruited in that county. In 1809, however, it became the Buckinghamshire Regiment due to a mutual swap of titles agreed by the Colonels of the 14th and the 16th Foot. By 1869, though, its depot was in Chatham in Kent and it was recruiting from there. A few years later its depot moved to Bradford and, as a result of the 1881 reorganization of the army, it was named the West Yorkshire Regiment.

1. *The Nature of Military Collections*

For nearly two and a half centuries the army had been nurtured on traditions that found their origins in the even more remote past. The process has tended to preserve the visible relics of those bygone days without seeking to examine the conditions in which they came into being.

(H.G. De Watteville 1954:233)

We all know, or think we know, what to expect when we walk into a military museum. There will be glass cases full of weapons, uniforms and badges[1]. The walls will be hung with tattered flags and paintings of martial glory (Figure 1.1) and in the courtyard will stand a huge gun or tank. Yet perhaps it is less obvious how these objects came together in the first place. A knowledge of the origins of these collections is, I believe, of vital importance in understanding the nature of military museums and the way in which military history is portrayed in them.

In the study of collecting it can be argued (Pearce 1991) that there are four main types of collections – relics, souvenirs, fetish collections, and true collections – and I shall be returning to these later. But in the study of military collections I think we have to be aware of two other potent forces behind this acquisition process: accidental accumulation and looting.

Amongst the assemblages of militaria found in this country are those which take the form of the neatly arranged circles of pistols or pikes which decorate the walls of stately homes, alongside the obligatory suits of armour. Admittedly some of these collections were acquired during the Victorian or Edwardian eras to add charm to these houses, but the true origin of such collections lies in the requirement for the landed nobility to provide a small army of their retainers and tenants to defend their county or country from foreign invaders or civil strife. They purchased arms and equipment for these retainers and stored them in readiness for the day they would be needed. The day may never have come, but the weapons remained in store or on the walls of the state-rooms providing the raw materials for the later decorative flourishes of interior designers.

Perhaps the most famous example of this type of accidental accumulation is the Royal Armouries in the Tower of London, where the armour and weapons for the monarch's army were stored. This collection became so large and famous that in the 1680s it was opened to the public. A similar accidental accumulation happened at the

Figure 1.1   Main hall of the Royal Scots Regimental Museum prior to refurbishment.
Its display was typical of a number of regimental museums.
Source: Royal Scots Regimental Museum

Woolwich Arsenal, where new guns were tested in the seventeenth and
eighteenth centuries and where men were trained to use them. Within
a short time a collection of obsolete pieces had accumulated which was
to form the basis of the Royal Regiment of Artillery's Museum of
Artillery.

At Bovington Camp in Dorset the prototype of the tank was tested
and the area around the camp remained a tank testing ground during
and after the First World War. By 1923 the camp had accumulated a
unique collection of prototype and early operational tanks which were
rusting in the open. Rudyard Kipling, on a visit to the camp, expressed
regret that this fine collection was being allowed to rot, and from this
observation grew the idea of forming the Tank Museum (Brown
1960:75).

formation of a large collection explains the origins of the Weapons
Museum at the School of Infantry at Warminster and the small-arms
collection in the Pattern Room at Nottingham, as well as the regimental
badge proof collection at the Imperial War Museum and the ship model
collections in the National Maritime Museum and the Royal Naval
Museum.

But, of course, the accidental survival of objects accounts for more
than just the existence of the occasional large collection of weapons.
Small collections, or indeed single objects, can survive in this way
and owe their eventual place in a museum to this happy chance. In the
British Army, for example, until the twentieth century officers were
required to purchase their own uniforms and equipment, including
their sword, and many also purchased firearms for their own protection. When they left the army these accoutrements went with them, to
be used in civilian life, discarded or stored. Often, as this privately
purchased clothing and equipment was of the best quality available at
the time, it has survived to the present day in good condition.

The private soldier, on the other hand, was usually issued with his
uniform and equipment, which was likely to be of much poorer quality.
He was also expected to use it until it was worn out or was unserviceable
before a replacement was issued[2]. Indeed, a soldier's uniform was likely
to have had far more wear than that of an officer, because officers seldom
wore their uniforms when not on duty, whereas soldiers, lacking the
luxury of several suits of clothes, generally wore theirs both on and
off duty. When the soldier subsequently left the army he was rarely able
to take any of this equipment with him, with the exception perhaps of
the last uniform he wore, and he was less likely than the officer to have
other clothes or boots to wear in his new civilian occupation. It is small
wonder, therefore, that, until the nineteenth century, when the overall
quality of uniforms improved and the introduction of military pensions
meant that some private soldiers would not have to work again after
service, so few uniforms of other ranks survived.

Happenstance can also affect, of course, the particular nature of
the material which survives. Officers, particularly in Wellington's army,
would often go into battle wearing sturdy civilian clothes or some
mixture of civilian dress and military uniform, as a tableau in the National
Army Museum shows. If they died of disease or were killed in action
during a campaign, they would probably be buried in this makeshift
uniform. If they survived, these civilian clothes or worn out campaign
uniforms would be more likely than their dress uniforms to be thrown
away. This partly accounts for the preponderance of the heavily embell-
ished parade uniforms which fill the glass cases in military museums,
giving a misleading impression of what soldiers really wore.

This kind of accidental survival also affects social history museums,
and perhaps all other museums, to a greater or lesser extent. It would
not be worth discussing here except that military museums are often
accused of only representing the lives of officers in their displays, and
of ignoring the daily lives of the private soldiers. This is undoubtedly

true in some cases, but it must also be recognized that the majority of museums of all types build their displays around the objects they have in their collections. Military museums are no exception, and the equipment and uniforms of officers are much more likely to have survived than those of the other ranks, for the reasons outlined above. In 1971, for example, the National Army Museum had more officers' coats from the eighteenth century alone than there were other ranks' coats in its collection from all other battles before Balaclava in 1854 (Reid 1971:63). In the case of the Navy, while officers began wearing standardized uniforms in 1748, sailors were not likely to be issued with a uniform before the middle of the nineteenth century.

It is hardly surprising, therefore, that the material culture of officers should be over-represented in these displays, or that the pomp and circumstance of military life should be featured at the expense of the harsh reality of the serviceman's existence.

Looting may also have led to the accidental survival of objects. It was a form of theft, of course, and as such was usually frowned upon by the military authorities. Yet in the past it has often been the main stimulus for military activities. The early Viking raids on Britain were for plunder, as were most of the great adventures of the English sea-dogs in the sixteenth century. And Napoleon Bonaparte took advantage of his campaigns in Italy and elsewhere to accumulate numerous treasures for France and for himself (Lewis 1992a:11).

Looting is often graced with the term 'living off the land', and is used to justify the theft of food and other essential supplies from the local population. Indeed, throughout history, in most military campaigns one or both of the rival armies have had to rely on this form of semi-official theft to survive. In the same vein, the seizure of the arms and equipment of the enemy has been recognized as a legitimate target and campaign aim. Less readily accepted has been the looting of civilians' houses when cities, ports or other settlements have been captured, though often such looting has been seen as a reward for the soldiers' or sailors' efforts, or was believed to be uncontrollable, and so their commanders turned a blind eye (Turner 1956:148–9).

Clearly, such looting has usually been of consumables like food and clothing and strong liquor. But often objects looted by soldiers or sailors while on campaign were taken because of their intrinsic value or because they could be of permanent use to the individual or unit. The officers' mess might accumulate cooking utensils, cutlery or glass-ware or even more exotic objects. Some of these would later acquire the status of souvenirs, and indeed souvenirs and useful objects might well be acquired at the same time. But, no matter what the similarity of the eventual fate of these objects and that of the souvenirs taken at the same time, it is important to stress that they owe their original accumulation to a very different urge. Thus while the caravans which Field Marshal Viscount Montgomery of Alamein captured from his Italian opponents during the desert campaign in the Second World War and had converted to his own use, and which now sit in the

Imperial War Museum, may have eventually come to act as a souvenir of his wartime service, their original acquisition owed nothing to sentiment.

It may seem that this differentiation between loot and souvenir is of little importance. Yet it must play a part in the way such objects are interpreted in a museum context. Objects which were originally acquired as loot can throw considerable light onto the way in which servicemen lived while on campaign, or demonstrate clearly what material things they valued and were willing to carry with them.

Military museums also contain objects which fall more easily into the accepted classifications for collections[3]. Relics constitute the first of these formal divisions. They are said to embody the religious experience of the community. The medieval world was apparently knee-deep in the relics of saints, martyrs and holy men, but such relics have been out of fashion in Britain since the Reformation and it may seem highly unlikely that such a concept should be applicable to the armed forces. Yet it needs hardly any stretch of the imagination, or any abuse of the term 'relic', to find within some military collections objects or groups of objects which could qualify as such. On display in the National Maritime Museum, for example, is the bloodstained and damaged coat in which Admiral Lord Horatio Nelson died in 1805. Similar personal objects relating to that great man appear in the Royal Naval Museum at Portsmouth. The Royal Engineers Museum at Chatham has an extensive collection of objects on display which once belonged to General Charles Gordon, including his full regalia as a mandarin presented to him by the Emperor of China (Figure 1.2), though some have no real military connection or significance. In the Hôtel des Invalides in Paris the hat, uniform and personal effects of Napoleon Bonaparte are displayed near his sarcophagus. In all these examples it is hard to escape the feeling that the motive for the retention and public display of these personal effects of the dead commander is little different from that which led to the accumulation and exhibition of relics of the saints in medieval times though perhaps the aim was to engender patriotism or military pride rather than religious fervour. Indeed, the Royal Naval Museum describes the personal effects of Nelson as having been 'carefully preserved almost like holy relics' (White 1989:9)).

In military circles other inanimate objects can achieve a significance similar to that of a holy relic. The flag, or 'colour', of the army regiment originally had a practical use in warfare. It acted as a means of identifying the unit. The colour was therefore paraded in front of the troops so that they would recognize it and be able to rally to it in battle. From this comes the ceremony of Trooping the Colour. But the colour acquired much more significance than just being a unit logo. Like the unit badge, it symbolizes the unit, indeed it comes to represent its soul. To lose its colours to the enemy was, therefore, one of the greatest disgraces that a military unit could suffer, and when a colour is retired or a unit disbanded, the old colour is often hung in the unit's local church as though to emphasize its quasi-religious nature. It is little

Figure 1.2 Dragon robe belonging to General Charles Gordon, part of the set of
Chinese court dress with which he was invested after his successful
campaign against the Tai Ping rebellion, 1860–1864.
Source: Royal Engineers Museum

wonder that representations of soldiers either saving their own colours,
as in a tableau in the Regiments of Gloucestershire Museum and one
in the Royal Scots Regimental Museum, or capturing enemy colours,
like a painting in the Royal Scots Dragoon Guards Museum, feature so
prominently in regimental museums.

Similar significance is often given to the regiment's book of the
fallen or to its collection of medals, particularly its Victoria Crosses
and other gallantry awards. Such medal galleries, of which particularly
good examples can be seen in the Royal Marines Museum and in the
Durham Light Infantry Museum (Figure 1.3), may also include the
colours or the roll of honour, and are often referred to, or at least
thought of, as the regiment's 'shrine'.

It is not surprising that such religious symbolism should surround
some key military artifacts, as death is a constant element of military life,

Figure 1.3 Medal Gallery of the Durham Light Infantry Museum.
Source: Durham Light Infantry Museum and Arts Centre

and these symbols help to commemorate those of the regiment who
have died. But there is more to it than that. Symbolism plays a large part
in the life of most military units. In army regiments in particular a great
deal of emphasis is placed on the idea of the regiment being a family.
There is clearly an important practical as well as emotional element to
this. Men are taken from civilian life, sometimes, particularly in the
past, against their will, and within a short time they have to be welded
into a unit which can work and live successfully together for many years.
Moreover, they are expected to face extreme hardship, danger and
death at the command of a senior member of the regiment. Obviously,
obedience of this kind can be secured with the threat of severe punishment. But fear alone will not produce the courage and comradeship
needed for a unit to function effectively in peace and war.

For this the unit has to achieve a true unity, like a family. In a close
family people accept the authority of the father and mother figures; they
will make allowances for each others' weaknesses and will pull together
in hard times. They will even, when the need arises, lay down their lives
for other members of the family. Over and over again the similarity
of the regiment or the ship to a close-knit family is emphasized in unit
literature, through legends and stories or through symbols whose

meaning is shared by all members of the family but which may be meaningless to outsiders. One example of this symbolism is shown in the 'Salt Ceremony', an old custom of the East Surrey Regiment (which is now part of the Princess of Wales's Royal Regiment). It is perpetuated by each officer on first dining in the regiment (and, of course, eating together is one of the most common bonding ceremonies in a family). The officer is required to take salt from a special cellar which contains a fragment of the Regimental Colour of the 31st Regiment (from whom the East Surreys originated) inside its cover. The buff cloth of the colour is revealed when the salt is taken, and the officer is then reminded of his responsibilities to the regiment (Griffin 1985:73).

This kind of symbolism can also attach to some objects which should be described as souvenirs rather than relics. Souvenirs can be defined as those pieces which encapsulate memories and experiences. They exist not in their own right, but because they represent or symbolize times past. They act as triggers for narrative and they are used to demonstrate the truth of that narrative (Pearce 1991:19). In the case of military souvenirs, some at least were acquired as loot. A few, as has been noted above, will have had an obvious practical purpose to begin with but will have acquired a more symbolic meaning later. In 1898, for example, a Royal Engineers Telegraph detachment was operating from the Dongola telegraph office during the reconquest of the Sudan. When the time came to withdraw from the area, Lieutenant A.H. Bagnold RE 'liberated' the office clock and arranged to have it brought back to England, where it was set up in the Officers' Mess of the Signal Training Centre. It functioned as the mess clock for the next 60 years, even suffering the indignity of having its original mechanism replaced twice: once with a similar mechanism in 1926, and again in the early 1960s with an electric one. Yet, at some time in its early life in the mess, it was fitted with brass plates on which were inscribed the names of all the officers who had served in the Telegraph Battalion between 1870 and 1914, and a list of all the theatres of war in which they had operated. It had thus been given at the same time both a practical purpose and a symbolic one (Thwaites 1992:15).

Other objects in military collections have had a similar dual purpose, though some are more clearly souvenirs than the Dongola Clock. During the Indian Mutiny in 1857, for example, the 1st Battalion of the Black Watch took a brass gong from the mutineers of the Gwalior contingent at Seraghai, while the 2nd Battalion was the first unit of the Mesopotamian Expeditionary Force to enter Baghdad in March 1917, capturing a bell at Samarra Railway Station in the process. Both these souvenirs have been used for many years to sound time in the Black Watch barracks (Griffin 1985:158).

Perhaps a more famous souvenir, which is still used by the regiment, is the King's Royal Hussars' loving cup, called 'the Emperor'. After the Battle of Vittorio in 1813 during the Peninsular War, the 14th Light Dragoons captured a coach belonging to Joseph Bonaparte, brother of Napoleon, and inside they found a silver chamber pot bearing the arms of Imperial France. Since that time, on guest nights in the regiment's Officers' Mess, after the loyal toast and a toast to the health of the regiment's Colonel-in-Chief, the mess sergeant brings in the chamber pot (the Emperor), filled with champagne, and it is passed around as a loving cup, with all those who drink from it for the first time being given thunderous applause. 'When all have drunk, the commanding officer directs the mess sergeant to invite one or more of the officers dining to finish off the Emperor, and the last one, who might be the last joined subaltern or an officer about to retire, to hold it upside down over his head on completion' (Dickinson 1973:34). This souvenir plays a part, therefore, in a mess ceremony which helps to cement that particular family together.

It is not only such regimental souvenirs which can have this kind of mixture of symbolic and practical application. After the Battle of Maida in July 1806, Lieutenant Colonel James Kempt made his supper off a tortoise and saved the shell as a memento. Later it was mounted in silver as a snuff box for his mess, and is now in the historic collection of the Queen's Lancashire Regiment. In that way it has or had a practical use while still reminding members of the regiment of the exploits of one of its officers (Griffin 1985:146).

Not all souvenirs are, of course, either so practical or so official. Many of those which now lie in military museums originally formed part of the collection of private mementos of a member of the regiment. Some, of course, should still be classified as loot. Liberated silver cups and candelabra abound in museum collections, as well as captured weapons, flags and uniforms. Yet there are also curious examples of souvenirs acquired through vandalism or salvage. The Guards Museum, for example, has a piece of the lock and chain and fragments of the wood taken from the principal gate of Hougomont Farm at Waterloo and garden ornaments from Napoleon's head-quarters at Le Caillow. The Regimental Museum of the 9th/12th Royal Lancers boasts a piece of the Lucknow Gate broken off during the Indian Mutiny in 1857, and a box made from timber from the Lucknow Residency now lies in the National Army Museum. Both the Royal Naval Museum and the National Maritime Museum hold a number of examples of boxes, tables and other objects made from the timbers of British or enemy naval ships, while the Royal Warwickshire Regimental Museum even has a piece of the wooden casing of the Mahdi's tomb, probably originally seized in the course of an orgy of destruction and souvenir hunting.

Perhaps the strangest of these souvenirs are those objects which would now be classified as ethnographic. Soldiers and sailors have always brought back curios from their foreign campaigns or voyages. Such items appeared amongst the offerings in Roman temples and in the collections of eighth-century caliphs (Lewis 1992a:6). British military museums now have their fair share.

The collection of the King's Regiment (Liverpool), now housed in the Liverpool Museum, for example, boasts a number of such items.

Amongst the mementos of Colonel A.S. de Peyster[4], who commanded the regiment for ten years towards the end of the eighteenth century, are ornaments of beads and skin and a tom-tom presented to him by North American Indians. He also received after a 'pow-wow' a peace-pipe and ceremonial hatchet, as well as an otter-skin tobacco pouch from the ruling chief. His collection also contains a white beaver skin which, like any good souvenir, supports a story told about the Colonel. Legend has it that a certain Sioux chief declared that a spirit came to him in the form of a white beaver and told him to kill Colonel de Peyster. When the good Colonel heard this, he demanded that the chief should bring him the white beaver pelt and thus save his own skin. The chief did as he was told, and the skin became one of the Colonel's souvenirs (Heughan 1934:423–4).

That regiment's collection also includes the golden umbrella which King Theebaw of Burma had carried over his head as a symbol of his kingship. When he surrendered to the British in 1885, he presented this object to Colonel A.A. le Messurier who was commanding the 2nd Battalion of the King's Regiment. A similar symbol of kingship is held in the Royal Signals Museum in Blandford. In 1896 a British force was sent into Ashanti in West Africa and deposed King Prempeh. The king's throne chair (Figure 1.4) was presented to the commander of the Telegraph detachment, Major (later Major General Sir Reginald) Curtis, by the British general in recognition of the important service rendered during the campaign by that unit. In 1921 Curtis presented this war trophy to the Royal Signals Officers' Mess, where it remained until 1962 when it was passed to the museum (Thwaites 1992:20).

Another chair said to have belonged to King Prempeh is amongst the collection of Ashanti trophies captured by the West Yorkshire Regiment which now resides in the Leeds City Museum, while the National Army Museum has a ceremonial execution bowl, trumpet and drum from the Ashanti king's palace, taken at the same time. The King's Own Royal Regiment collection in the Lancaster City Museum has a number of religious artifacts taken from Magdala during the 1868 Abyssinian Campaign, and the Royal Naval Museum has a carved wooden statue of a warrior or god captured during the Gambian Expedition of 1892. Many other military collections hold exotic curios of this nature. They are not, of course, prized for their own intrinsic symbolic value. Indeed, in most cases, it is doubtful whether the soldier who stole, confiscated, found or purchased the particular item knew or was interested in its original religious or cultural meaning and significance. It was merely a souvenir which reminded him of a campaign, or a posting, or a specific incident, and it is for that reason that it has been preserved and has become a regimental treasure.

Obviously it would be quite wrong to suggest that such exotic and ethnographic items make up more than just a small proportion of the souvenirs which are found in military collections. The majority more closely resemble the Queen's Lancashire Regiment's tortoise-shell snuff box. Examples abound of cigarette lighters and letter openers made

Figure 1.4 King Prempeh's chair: an Ashanti War trophy of the Royal Engineers Telegraph Battalion.
Source: Royal Signals Museum

from bullets, and ashtrays fabricated from shell cases. The Royal Marines Museum, for instance, has a paper knife made from the wood of HMS *Tremendous*, while the King's Own Royal Regiment collection holds a letter box made from the breech block of a Boer Pom-Pom gun retrieved by Captain J.M.A. Graham of that regiment. Moreover, items like Lieutenant Henry Anderson's coatee from the Battle of Waterloo, now held in the National Army Museum, or Major Thomas Waters's sea chest and uniform, which are among the holdings of the Royal Marines Museum, must also have had 'the value and emotional tone of a souvenir' (Pearce 1990:127), and that is why they were kept by their original owner and treasured by his descendants.

Such items are redolent of acts of personal bravery, close encounters with death and the endurance of hardship. They take their place along-side captured weapons, enemy helmets and cigarette cases pierced by bullets to illustrate tales of battles and campaigns. As Professor Pearce has argued (1990:127), for the first person who cherished such objects they 'probably represented a time when life seemed more exciting and more meaningful than the dull present of middle age'. They would also serve, she adds, 'to sum up, or make coherent in personal and small scale terms, an important event which seemed confused, spasmodic and incoherent to most of the individuals who took part in it'. Finally, such objects act 'as the personal validation of a personal narrative'.

But, of course, the serviceman's life was not all battles and scrapes with death, and souvenirs reflect this. Some of the ethnographic items we have examined reflect the experience of foreign travel, and may well be supported by such unmilitary artifacts as prints of local scenes and other tourist items. The family life that he left behind is often reflected in the portrait miniatures or, in a later period, the family photographs which he carried with him, or by some personal item of kit. An example of this is the handmade holdall, decorated with hearts and probably the work of his wife or sweetheart, used during military service from 1843 by Private Vaughan of the 4th Foot, which now lies near Captain Graham's breech block letter-box in the King's Own Royal Regiment Museum.

Other personal items and mementos abound, like the King's Own Royal Regiment Museum's Boer War collection of hard tack biscuit, chocolate gift box, sealed emergency rations and knife, fork and spoon set, the Boer War pipe in the Museum of the Manchesters and the collection of sporting equipment in the Museum of the King's Regiment (Liverpool). Such artifacts may now tell us a lot about the social history of the armed forces, as we shall see in Chapter 5, but they probably owe their survival to the nostalgic connotations that they had for a particular serviceman or for his family.

As well as these artifacts, another group of items must be counted as souvenirs, though they are perhaps less obvious candidates for that title. These are the documentary records and personal papers kept by servicemen from their periods of service. Most military collections, as will be shown in Chapter 8, contain examples of enlistment forms, paybooks, records of service, discharge papers, pension books and other official documents which chart servicemen's military life in brief official language. Along with these will be the rarer examples of soldiers' and sailors' diaries or letters and personal memoirs, which often give a graphic account of their experiences. On the face of it these items may not appear to be souvenirs, but they usually owe their survival to the instinct which causes an ex-serviceman to keep his knife, fork and spoon set, or the bullet which nearly killed him.

Of course if he has kept every bullet and shell case that he ever came upon during his military service, or every beer-mat or postcard, then it may well be that other instincts apart from nostalgia were playing a part here. Such collecting will probably fall under the third main classification of collection, the 'fetish', where the intention is to gather as many examples of a particular class of material as possible. As Professor Pearce (1989:7) has noted: 'Accumulations formed in this style are essentially different from souvenirs, in that fetishes do not have an historical but more-or-less fortuitous link with personal experience, but rather are deliberately acquired by somebody who already knows that something in his nature will respond to them'; the aim is 'to acquire as many samples of the admired material as possible'.

Undoubtedly some of the items held in military museums came about through this kind of collecting. The Royal Military Academy Sandhurst Museum acquired on its formation in the early 1950s a collection of military prints, pictures and porcelain figures which had originally been put together by Colonel C. de W. Crookshank (Boultbee 1951:16) which might fall into this category. Other military museums hold assemblages of tin soldiers or military vehicle models which had previously been the property of individuals, and might have counted as fetish collections, while some of the collections of badges, medals or uniform accoutrements they boast could owe their origin to a similar urge.

It is often difficult to differentiate between these fetish collections and the so-called organized collections which form the last major division of military (and other) collections, particularly once they have been in a museum for a number of years and may have become divided up or rearranged, losing their original context. The organized collections are formed 'to demonstrate a particular intellectual concept, and for that reason they operate by gathering examples (rather than many samples) of all the artifacts which form part of the given intellectual rationale' (Pearce 1991:19). In this way, what I have previously described as accidental accumulations have often been developed into organized collections by a deliberate policy of acquisition. The originally accidental accumulation of tanks at Bovington Camp, for example, has been built up over the years into a comprehensive collection, reflecting the development and use of tanks by Britain and by the other major military powers, while the small-arms collection in the Weapons Museum at Warminster and the gun collection in the Museum of Artillery at Woolwich have been similarly augmented. Collections like these have often been seen as valuable teaching aids, allowing trainees and recruits to see how particular weapons or systems have developed over time[5]. But whether this has been the cause of or the retrospective justification for their accumulation is a moot point.

In general, such collections have seemed to be the most obvious ones for military museums to build up. Many of the souvenir items and relics I have discussed would have formed part of the decoration of the mess or the private home of the individual, but in the regimental stores would have been found examples of uniforms, buttons, weapons and equipment which were obsolete but had not been destroyed because they formed part of the unit's inventory and had not yet been written off. Moreover, in modern times, at least, units have been able to 'bid' for examples of such standard equipment, when they are declared obsolete by the Ministry of Defence, to add to their museum or training collections.

It has in any case seemed the kind of collection that military museums should hold. Charles ffoulkes, the first Curator and Secretary of the Imperial War Museum, argued in 1918, for example, that this new national museum should 'exhibit a complete series of weapons of war which will be of practical technical interest to the student of military matters' (ffoulkes 1918:59). Similarly, when reviewing the latest list of items which had been donated to the nascent Royal Signals Museum in 1943, Major General C.W. Fladgate, the Director of Signals, asked if the museum was really intended to include the 'considerable quantity of junk such as old weapons which have no technical interest or associ-ation' that appeared on the list of museum holdings. He argued instead in favour of building up 'a complete sequence of equipment, rather like making up a stamp collection', and it was later suggested by his colleagues on the Royal Signals Corps Committee that the Officers' Mess might be a more suitable repository than the museum for medals and other personal items (Thwaites 1992:11). It may be that this partly reflected the bias of a technical arm of the army which was proud of, and wished to stress in its public display, technical expertise. But I suspect that this emphasis on building up collections of equipment is also typical of the way in which many soldiers have until recently viewed their historic collections.

Indeed, much of the criticism which has been heaped onto military museums in the past has related to their insistence on showing off their highly organized collections of such things as buttons, badges, gorgets, hats and weapons to a public which had neither the knowledge, interest or patience to appreciate the subtle differences being demonstrated between the examples on display (Wood 1986b and 1987a). But military displays are changing, and such organized collections are now more likely to be found in the museum store, where they can be examined by the expert and the enthusiast, than in the galleries.

On the other hand, one traditional element in the military collection, which could be called the 'artificial relic', is still very much in evidence in modern military exhibitions. I am referring to paintings and silver centrepieces. These works of art have elements both of relics or souvenirs and of organized collections. At one level, they have the essence of a relic because they depict or represent either the great military figures or the great acts of bravery associated with a particular unit, and they usually show or record the unique and the special rather than the ordinary and mundane. They are not, therefore, innocent, or even always accurate, historical records, but help, like relics or souvenirs, to support stories or perpetuate legends.

At the same time they have elements of the organized collection for, while many of these paintings and works in silver were commissioned as spontaneous reactions to particular events, there is a tendency amongst regiments to ensure that most historical periods and major events are recorded with a suitable painting or centrepiece. So that new works are commissioned to mark modern events or to fill in gaps in the historical record, and, while the silver will be intended for use in the mess on special occasions, it often resides in the museum, helping to illustrate the unit's history. The Royal Green Jackets Museum, for instance, has a fine collection of regimental silver in its 'Regimental Uniforms and Personalities' display, and most military museums have regimental history paintings on their walls.

In this chapter I have discussed the very different types of material which make up military collections for the period of this study. Of course, they are now usually mixed together within display cases or stores, but the way these military collections developed was determined to some extent by the circumstances in which they were originally brought together.

Most of the accidental collections remain in stately homes or royal castles, because that is where they were stored for use. The personal souvenirs, fetish collections and some of what could be termed the relics, on the other hand, resided in the family homes of the individuals to whom they belonged until an appeal for objects for the museum drew them back to the regiment. Their survival largely depended, therefore, on their having some sentimental value for the family of the original owner, or, as a caption in the Royal Naval Museum explains in relation to relics from the Battle of Trafalgar, on their being connected to some event of obvious national importance. Moreover, to have remained in the personal collection of a family for perhaps many generations, it is unlikely that such objects would be very large or very fragile! The organized collections of equipment and uniform accoutrements usually languished in the unit store until the decision was taken to turn them into museum objects. Their survival would, therefore, have often depended on the vagaries of official policy with regard to surplus kit, and on the lucky chance that they were held in a large or disorganized store. It is not often, under these circumstances, that perfect series of types of arms or equipment would have survived.

Until the twentieth century the majority of the relics, souvenirs, artificial relics and many of the other historical artifacts now in military museums would have formed part of the decoration of the regiment's messes, alongside hunting and sporting trophies.

The officers' mess is a relatively modern institution. Before the late eighteenth century soldiers were lodged in barns and inns and they did not eat together as a regiment except in a disorganized way when on campaign. Officers in some regiments did enjoy a measure of communal life in local taverns, but 'by no means all regiments kept up an officers' mess as it would be recognised today' (Turner 1956:84). The threat of invasion by the French at the end of that century, however, resulted in the need to concentrate troops together in strategic places, which in turn led to the building of barracks. Officers could not, of course, eat or sleep in the same places as their men without seriously undermining discipline, or so it was believed at the time. Moreover, the class divide between officers and men was so large that it is unlikely that either would have felt comfortable in the others' company in a social context. Because of this, separate rooms were set aside where the officers could eat and relax together, within the barracks but out of sight of the other ranks. Within a short time similar messes were set up for the senior non-commissioned officers and, later, for the corporals.

The messes quickly became established, therefore, as the centre of the social life of the regiment. Equally importantly, they came to be the place where the spirit of the regiment resided. We have already mentioned one mess ceremony relating to the King's Royal Hussars' loving cup, 'the Emperor'. Each regiment has its own ceremonies surrounding the taking of meals, the drinking of toasts and the playing of games in the mess, which help to initiate the newcomer and bind the regiments' officers or non-commissioned officers into as close a family unit as possible (Dickinson 1973).

Part of this process of helping to socialize the newcomer and of maintaining the regiment's cohesion and pride in itself took the form of decorating the mess with the unit's trophies. These were often, as suggested above, hunting and sporting trophies which helped to demonstrate the skill and prowess of past and current members of the unit. But pride of place was usually given to historic relics and souvenirs, while the walls would be decorated with the paintings and the tables with the silver centrepieces which recorded or depicted the brave deeds of the regiment and of the individual men who served in it (Moss 1970:1 and Dickinson 1973:29).

For 150 years, therefore, these messes, either situated in the regiment's home depot or travelling with the individual battalion to its overseas postings, acted as a kind of regimental museum as well as a social centre. It is important to remember that these collections had a decorative as well as a training and inspirational function, which almost certainly had some influence on which historic items survived and which did not. Moreover, these messes were not open to the public and the historic objects they contained were used to interpret the regiment's history in a particular way for its own members, for important civilian guests or for visiting representatives of other regiments. Clearly, what needed to be emphasized were the glorious achievements of the regiment. While it was acceptable, therefore, to record the bravery and hardship endured by its members, it was unlikely that either its failures or the more general history of the campaigns in which it was involved would be recorded. Nor was it likely that the more mundane features of army life would be commemorated in its decoration or in the symbolic objects it chose to treasure. Indeed large, ugly, mundane or ordinary objects were likely to be discarded.

This has had, of course, a profound effect on the character and balance of the historic artifacts which have survived, and on the nature of the historical record they can recount. As has already been suggested, the artifacts of army officers were more likely to survive than those of their men, and army relics will easily outnumber those of the navy for the reasons outlined in the Introduction. But, just as importantly, the special was more likely to survive than the mundane, the small and hardy rather than the large or fragile, and the records of successes rather than those of failures. While the story of the regiment was just for the consumption of its own members, this imbalance was hardly of any great importance. Indeed, until the 1920s the British Army showed little inclination to share its legends and stories with anyone else. Why this changed in the years after the First World War, leading to the plethora of military museums we see in Britain today, will be considered in the next chapter, while the implications for these museums of the gaps in regimental collections will become clear in later chapters.

Notes

1. 'It is not often appreciated that lack of storage space, combined with an attempt to impress the visitor often leads to these over full cases' (Westrate 1961:6).
2. Captain D. Horn, Curator of the Guards Museum, quoted in *Focus*, the MoD house magazine, March 1993, p.20.
3. The classifications used in this section are based on those given in Pearce (1991:19).
4. Colonel de Peyster's collection was originally donated to the Dumfries and Maxwelltown Observatory in his home town of Dumfries and purchased by the regiment in 1933, a year before its museum opened.
5. See for example the *Guide for the Weapons Museum* (1984), Warminster, The School of Infantry, p.11.

2. The Formation of Military Museums

In order to understand the army of today, or still more in the future, it would be as well to obtain a clearer insight into how our soldiers have been treated in peace and employed in war in their past history.

(H.G. De Watteville 1954:234)

The Royal Armouries in the Tower of London first opened to the public in the 1680s, and so can lay claim to being the oldest public museum in Britain, though that honour is usually reserved for the Ashmolean Museum in Oxford (Lewis 1992a:10). The magnificent collection on display, which has been growing ever since, tells the story of the development of the arms and armour used in this country since medieval times. It could be enjoyed by those interested in the technical aspects of arms and armour and by those who appreciated the artistic merit of these handcrafted artifacts. But the Royal Armouries were not intended as a museum of the general military history of this country, nor did their foundation lead to a spate of other military collections being opened to the public. It was, indeed, nearly 100 years later before another military museum was formed, though this is perhaps not surprising as at that time museums were still a rarity.

By 1778 a large collection of guns and other artillery equipment had accumulated at the Royal Arsenal at Woolwich. King George III saw the value for training purposes of having many types of guns and their equipment together in one place, and he ordered that a Museum of Artillery should be set up on the site. When established it formed part of the Royal Military Repository where training in the handling of all types of artillery equipment was carried out. In 1802, fire completely destroyed the original building and so the collection was moved up the hill to a site near the Royal Artillery Barracks. The collection was rehoused in a huge tent which had previously been used for a meeting of the Allied sovereigns after the fall of France in 1815. The tent was erected on its present site in 1820 and a lead roof was placed over it. In 1973 this tent had to be replaced by a replica during extensive repair work to the roof, but the unique design of the building was retained (Hughes 1975) (Figure 2.1).

The Museum of Artillery collection has continued to grow ever since its foundation, augmented by both obsolete British weapons and captured guns, so that it is now a very comprehensive collection of artillery pieces and related equipment from the fourteenth century to the present day (Figure 2.2). But this was, and is, a museum of

Figure 2.1 Rotunda of the Museum of Artillery in Woolwich with its distinctive
             tent shape.
Source: Peter Thwaites

weapons, like the Tower Armouries, and did not deal in any detail
with either the history of the Royal Regiment of Artillery or that of the
men who served in it. It was not until 1946 that the Royal Artillery
Regimental Museum was set up in another part of Woolwich.

In 1801 the Royal Military College, Sandhurst, was founded and soon
became the home of some historic artifacts. Some kind of museum was
set up there, but it had disappeared along with all of its exhibits, except
for some fortification models, before the end of the century (Boultbee
1951).

Meanwhile, in 1829 a letter from 'an old Egyptian Campaigner'
appeared in the *United Service Journal* suggesting that a museum of
military history and science should be established. The idea gained royal
support (*NAM Annual Report* 1977–8:24), and in June 1831 the Naval and
Military Library and Museum was formed for the use of officers of the
regular and auxiliary forces, the East India Company land and sea forces
and attached civil functionaries. In 1860 it became the Royal United
Service Institution (RUSI) and was given the use of the Banqueting
House in Whitehall in 1871 in which to display its artifacts. Apparently
this collection of relics, which included naval and, later, air force
exhibits, as well as regimental material, was 'rather of a personal than
of a national character' (ffoulkes 1918:58). Lieutenant Colonel L.I.

Figure 2.2 Interior of the Rotunda showing part of the gun collection of the Museum of Artillery.
Source: Royal Artillery Historical Trust

Cowper (1935:46), in an article reviewing military museums in the *Museums Journal* in 1935 , also felt that its displays were too crowded, and claimed that 'the profusion of material . . . defeats its own ends, for owing to the number of regiments represented, no clear picture can be obtained of any of them'. W. A. Thorburn (1962:192), writing in the *Museums Journal* at the time of the demise of the RUSI Museum, pointed out that it had a quantity of important specimens, which were unfortunately indiscriminately exhibited among miscellaneous militaria, and that 'financial considerations . . . prevented any development along modern lines'. But, despite these numerous apparent faults, it was the major military museum in this country before the formation of the Imperial War Museum, and its collections remained on display for 90 years. In 1962, the government reclaimed the Banqueting House and the artifacts were dispersed, many going to the new National Army Museum in Sandhurst, which also received the bulk of the RUSI's manuscript collection in 1968.

The RUSI Museum may have been the major military museum of the nineteenth century, but other collections were being formed at that time, though they did not as yet constitute formal museums. In the latter half of the nineteenth century, for example, a small collection of Crimean War and Indian Mutiny relics accumulated in rooms in Bristol set aside for social gatherings of the local veterans of those campaigns, though it never became an established museum and seems to have disappeared during the First World War (Kavanagh 1994:20).

In 1875, however, the first true British regimental museum was set up by the Royal Engineers[1]. The origins of this Royal Engineers Museum lay, in fact, in lessons learnt in the Peninsular War. The officers of the Royal Engineers had found themselves faced with a number of tasks in that campaign for which they had not received adequate training. As a result it was decided to set up the Royal Engineers Establishment (later called the School of Military Engineering) at Chatham in 1812, under the direction of Major (later General Sir Charles) Pasley, to train its officers. Pasley set up Model Rooms 'to explain by appropriate models those useful operations of field engineering, which, from their magnitude, or the great expense that would be incurred, cannot conveniently be practised at this establishment'[2] (Figure 2.3).

By 1852 a number of supporting drawings, maps, reports and even war trophies had been added to the models, and a chapel in the barracks was converted into a large Model Room to replace the earlier rooms. The collection was now open to all Royal Engineers and to visiting officers from other arms or units.

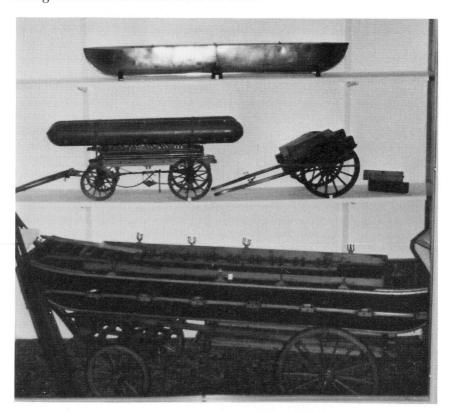

Figure 2.3   Training models in the Royal Engineers Museum. The one with the cylindrical floats (a Blanshard pontoon) was almost certainly one of the original artifacts in the School of Engineering Model Room.
Source: Royal Engineers Museum

In the meantime, in 1839, Sergeant Major J. Forbes had set up a museum in the Reading Room of the Non-Commissioned Officers' Library at the Woolwich Depot of the Royal Sappers and Miners, to hold 'Models, philosophical Apparatus, specimens of Natural History, Paintings etc'. This seems to have been something of a 'Cabinet of Curiosities', and in 1856, on the amalgamation of the Royal Engineers and the Royal Sappers and Miners, its collection was brought to Chatham and distributed between the Non-Commissioned Officers' Library, the Mess and the Model Room. In that way a number of Figi war clubs and spears, Japanese weapons, elephant tusks, Hindu sculptures and ancient Greek and Samarian sarcophagi and stoneware joined the plans, models and war trophies in the nascent museum.

In 1875 the Royal Engineers decided to set up their own Institute to look after the publication of their *Journal* and to oversee other technical matters. The officers of the Institute soon established a museum to 'illustrate the practical application of the arts and sciences as bearing on the duties of the Corps', taking as their lead the museums of other learned societies, and including in its collection fossils, rock specimens, minerals and stuffed birds. There were now, therefore, two rival museums in the same barracks, and in 1882 the Institute was also given control of the Model Room.

As these two museums were primarily designed as teaching aids, they were handed over to the School of Military Engineering in 1890. By 1902, however, they had fallen into disuse and the Model Room was being used for dances and concerts, with the exhibits pushed to one side or banished to the basement. But senior officers of the Corps decided in 1904 that the Corps needed a museum in which to exhibit its trophies and relics, and in 1910, having finally found an alternative site for the dances, the Model Room was converted into the museum and a paid curator was employed.

The Royal Engineers Museum which finally emerged in 1912 was set out in a way familiar to visitors to military museums today. It was based on the 'prime need for exhibiting trophies of the various campaigns, peace-time relics and old uniforms', and was laid out in a chronological sequence. Gradually, the geological and natural history specimens were cleared out and handed over to local museums and schools, though some of the exotic items from the original Non-Commissioned Officers' museum were kept as they bore 'testimony to the wide distribution of the Corps throughout the world'. In its first year it attracted 8,500 civilian visitors, and it continues to be a popular attraction.

No other regimental museums were founded in this country until after the First World War. But in the meantime an example was provided in Paris of a national museum devoted to the army. In 1905 in the Hôtel des Invalides the Museum of the Army was formed by the amalgamation of the Museum of the Artillery and the Ministry of War's Historical Museum, which contained a collection of military artifacts and 'relics' that had been accumulating since the late seventeenth century (Hudson 1987:115). It seems to act as a paean of praise to the glorious achievements of the French Army, and in particular to the Napoleonic Grand Army, which is perhaps not surprising in a building which also houses that emperor's mortal remains. This museum is said to have spawned only one direct imitator, in Belgium, but it established the precedent of a national museum devoted to the achievements of a national military force and to the commemoration of one of its leaders.

The greatest stimulus to the formation of military museums in Britain did not come, it seems, from this example, nor from the first tentative stirrings of a regimental museum in Chatham, nor even from the small Royal United Service Institution Museum. It came from the trauma of the First World War.

Even in its earliest days the First World War was clearly like no other war in which Britain had ever taken part. A huge number of men responded to the call for volunteers for the armed forces and a surge of patriotism and nationalist fervour swept the country. Although the forces which endured the hardship and casualties of the first few months of the war were the professionals of the Royal Navy and the tiny British regular army, it was not long before those who were suffering (and dying) were men and women who had been civilians before August 1914 and would be civilians again as soon as the war had ended. It was, therefore, a genuinely national war, particularly as so much of the population left in Britain also found themselves involved in war work in one form or another.

Not only was this the first total war but it was also the most intensively reported war up to that point. The Boer War had roused patriotic fervour and considerable interest, and war reports had been avidly read. But there was a far greater quantity of printed and photographic information coming back from the Western Front, supported by graphic newsreel footage. This, combined with the fact that within a short time virtually every family in Britain had a member serving in the armed forces, meant that people were well informed about this war and wanted to know even more. Moreover, the government was aware of the value of propaganda in promoting and maintaining morale, and encouraged and employed literary figures like George Bernard Shaw and John Masefield to visit the Front and write about what they saw (Kavanagh 1994:120).

Exhibitions of war material to help meet this public interest and to satisfy this thirst for knowledge began in late 1914 when the Science Museum brought together and exhibited a 'Warfare collection' of models of naval ships and military aircraft together with full-sized aircraft engines and examples of small arms and equipment. By 1915 Hull Museum was able to put on an exhibition of war mementos and souvenirs, and other exhibitions were organized by voluntary agencies like the Red Cross, by the national newspapers and by other commercial organizations.

These early displays tended to 'promote the war as an adventure, an exciting and necessary experience' (Kavanagh 1994:68). But as the number of war casualties rose to unprecedented levels and the mood of the country shifted from enthusiasm to apprehension, an increasing link was being made between war exhibitions and war memorials. This was particularly true of the art magazine *The Connoisseur*, edited by C. Reginald Grundy. Articles by Grundy and others appeared in 1915 and 1916 concerning war memorials or war mementos. But it was Grundy himself who made the first positive proposal on war museums.

In an article entitled 'Local War Museums' in the November 1916 edition of *The Connoisseur*, Grundy proposed that a war museum should be set up in every centre of population. These museums, he suggested, should contain rolls of honour, records of the local regiments and archives of press cuttings and photographs. This would be supported by uniforms, weapons, medals, souvenirs of the local officers and men who distinguished themselves, and mementos of local life during the war, as well as war trophies captured from the enemy. He believed that such local war museums would act as memorials to the local servicemen and would keep the events of the First World War fresh in the public memory and seize the imagination of posterity (*Museums Journal* 1917 16,9:219).

To promote the formation of local war museums, Grundy established a committee of museum curators, though this was later superseded by a much more high-powered Executive Committee of the Local War Museums Association set up in May 1917. The Executive Committee was assisted by a Museum Committee of professionals, which was active during the next eighteen months discussing the suggested philosophy for these local war museums and obtaining advice on the types of war trophies and souvenirs they should collect and display (see Leetham 1918:96).

But, as war weariness gripped the country in 1918, the idea of local war memorial museums became less and less attractive. Local authorities began to baulk at the likely cost of these new museums and the whole concept of a local museum just dedicated to commemorating the war was re-examined critically[3]. Other ways of commemorating the dead were found, including memorial gardens, crosses and sculptures, and, while in a few places museums or art galleries were built to act as war memorials, they did not take the form of war museums exhibiting the spoils of the First World War, but added instead to the town's or district's more traditional artistic or cultural provision. Moreover, the donations of personal souvenirs, war trophies and funds on which these museums would have depended just did not materialize. The Local War Museums Association folded soon after the end of the war, and within a comparatively short time the local collections of war material had either been disposed of, or had largely disappeared (Kavanagh 1994:112–13).

The local war museum idea had failed, but it had helped to spawn the rival idea of a National War Museum. Clearly Grundy and his colleagues had highlighted the idea that museum collections could be used as a way of commemorating this horrific war and remembering the sacrifice of those who had taken part in it. Gaynor Kavanagh also suggests that the government saw the propaganda value of setting up a war museum to commemorate the sacrifice made by the nation's servicemen and civilians at a time when the war was not going too well. Moreover, with the threat of competition from local war museums collecting war trophies, it was important that there should be a central organization able to select and acquire artifacts of national importance (Kavanagh 1994:122).

For whatever reasons, on 5 March 1917 the formation of the National (later to be retitled Imperial) War Museum was approved by the War Cabinet. This museum, the first of its kind in Western Europe, was intended to become the commemorative centre of the British Empire in relation to the war (though the idea of making it the national war memorial was opposed by the Cabinet, who felt it would be unsuitable). Sir Martin Conway, its first Director-General, felt that its most important function 'should be to serve as a laboratory for the many historians who in generations to come will fashion their histories of the Great War, and will trace down from these five fatal years the movements that will shape humanity throughout generations yet unborn'. He also hoped that it would help to prevent future wars, for, he argued, 'The wars of the future will not be waged by those who remember the strivings, the sufferings, the sacrifice, and the perils of the past. The danger is, not lest we too well remember, but "lest we forget"' (Conway 1920:28).

To help achieve his aims for the Imperial War Museum (IWM) Conway suggested that it should record and commemorate 'all activities called forth by the war at home, in the Dominions and in India, at all the fronts and on the sea' (quoted in Kavanagh 1994:130), which policy helped to give the museum its encyclopedic coverage of the First World War. He also argued that the IWM should absorb the post-1700 material held in the Royal United Service Institution Museum, and perhaps even some of the items held in the Royal Armouries at the Tower, so that its collections would then illustrate all the wars from the time of the Duke of Marlborough (Conway 1920:28). The Museum's first Curator and Secretary, Charles ffoulkes, who was concurrently the Curator of the Royal Armouries, had already suggested (ffoulkes 1918:59) that the IWM should absorb all military trophies from the nineteenth and twentieth centuries, and for the next ten years he continued to try to expand the terms of reference of the IWM to cover the history of armoury (Kavanagh 1994:145).

These ideas did not find favour with the Trustees of the Imperial War Museum or with the government, and the IWM's terms of reference were fixed at commemorating the First World War, though after 1939 they were extended to cover initially the Second World War, and finally all conflicts involving British or Commonwealth troops from 1914 to the present day. It could be argued, though, that an opportunity had been missed to form a comprehensive national military museum, similar to those found in Europe (see Westrate 1961), in which some of the topics not dealt with in our current military museums, such as the relationship between the armed forces and the civil state, could have been discussed.

Given the time period covered by the IWM, its collections fall outside the scope of this survey. But it is worth emphasizing some aspects of the story of the formation of the IWM which seem to have had a profound effect on the development of the other military museums in this country.

Firstly, although it had been not formed as a national military museum, but was intended instead to commemorate all aspects of the First World War, the IWM nevertheless included an important element of military history. It thus gave the concept of military history as a museum subject a much higher profile than the small RUSI Museum had ever been able to achieve. Secondly, although the local war museum concept had failed to take root, the travelling exhibitions of war paintings and relics sent out by the IWM in its first year of life may have helped to whet people's appetites for military history displays.

But, more importantly, the IWM was an all-service museum. It was trying to tell the whole history of the war, rather than the story of the achievements of particular military units, except, of course, when their exploits were central to this main theme. The local war museums, as we have seen, had been intended to record the war service of local units and of the local men who served in them. This was not the mandate or purpose of the IWM. Moreover, while ex-servicemen had shown a marked reluctance to donate their war trophies and souvenirs to these local war museums while the memories of the war were still fresh, it was likely that they would eventually want to find a home for them where they would be properly appreciated. The large and impersonal IWM may not have seemed the right place for them.

At the same time there seemed to be an overwhelming urge to record the part played in this war by particular units[4] and individuals. A plethora of books on the First World War were published, including the war histories of many of the units which had taken part in the conflict, as well as the memoirs of a large number of participants. Moreover, many individuals were finding that it was difficult to readjust to peacetime conditions. They could not put their wartime experiences behind them, and felt only really at home in the company of fellow ex-servicemen. Old comrades' associations flourished, and a considerable proportion of the visitors to the first home of the IWM were ex-servicemen (Kavanagh 1994:149).

It is perhaps not surprising, therefore, that the military units them-selves should begin to set up their own museums in which to hold their war trophies and in which to commemorate the achievements and sacrifices of their members. The first of these new regimental museums seems (Cowper 1935:42) to have been that of the East Yorkshire Regiment which was established in 1920[5]. By the end of 1929 there were 25 regimental and corps museums in Britain, and by 1935 this number had risen to 50. It must be admitted that some of them were pitifully small and poorly arranged (Figure 2.4), and most attracted few visitors

Figure 2.4. Interior (*c.* 1935) of an unnamed regimental museum in a depot
barracks showing a portion of the exhibits. It resembles a military store
and is unlikely to have been open to the public.
Source: Army Museums Ogilby Trust

(Cowper 1935:43), though the King's Own Royal Regiment Museum in
Lancaster had over 47,000 visitors a year. They had also been joined in
1930 by the Scottish National and Military Museum in Edinburgh Castle
which was later to acquire national museum status as the Scottish
United Services Museum, part of the National Museums of Scotland[6].

It is very tempting, then, to see this sudden wave of military museum
foundation as being entirely the result of the First World War and
of the commemorative urge which accompanied it. But the history
of these museums is not as simple as that. In the first place Gaynor
Kavanagh has argued that 'the four years of war had been a nightmare
and, with the peace, all effort was made to rub out its memory.
Conversation about the war died down even before the peace celebra-
tions. Soon books and articles about the War became unfashionable'
(Kavanagh 1984:69). Not the atmosphere it might be thought in which
to open 50 museums commemorating the very same war. The claim
that these museums were mainly commemorative might still hold
water if they had been established just for the use of the regiments
themselves or to cater for their ex-members. But by 1935 two-thirds of
these museums were already open to the general public, and, of those
which were not, most remained closed for practical reasons to do with
limited access or lack of funds, rather than because of the nature of
their displays.

In any case there is other evidence to suggest that these museums
were not primarily intended as memorials to the First World War. I have

not found, for example, a single case in which this has been put forward as the major reason for establishing a particular military museum by the museum itself. Moreover, the regimental Rolls of Honour are usually kept in the regimental church, not the museum, and while the medal gallery may act as a regimental shrine, it usually displays the medals of the living as well as the dead. In any case, a survey of the holdings and displays of even the earliest of the regimental and corps museums in the first years of their existence shows that they invariably covered the whole of the history of their regiment, with the First World War merely fitting in to this chronological story at the appropriate place[7]. Any preponderance it might have had in regimental displays seems to have been caused simply by the understandably greater availability of war trophies from that conflict, rather than as a result of any policy decision by the regimental authorities.

If, then, the purpose of opening these military museums was not primarily to commemorate the dead of the First World War (and indeed at least one military curator, that of the Queen's Own Royal West Kents' Regimental Museum, has argued forcibly that a museum cannot be a regimental shrine (quoted in Moss 1970:2)), what did cause this sudden explosion of military museums? One reason, as I have already argued, may well be the interest in military displays caused by the opening of the Imperial War Museum and by the travelling exhibitions it organized. The 1930s also saw an expansion in other areas of museum provision, though Gaynor Kavanagh has argued (1994:158) that at this time 'neither the mood nor the economy of the country was right for [the establishment of] formal regimental museums'. But the growth in military museums in this period may also have had rather more mundane and practical causes.

For over 100 years officers' and non-commissioned officers' messes had been receiving a steady stream of relics, trophies and artificial relics, and some of them were apparently running out of wall and floor space on which to display them (Pereira 1950:23). A fresh influx from the greatest war any of these regiments had experienced might have been too much. Clearly the core of most of the collections which appeared in these newly formed regimental museums had been held in their messes before, though they were soon supplemented by other historic items and personal souvenirs donated by ex-members of the regiments in response to appeals in the regimental magazines or local newspapers. In fact some historic items, like the King's Royal Hussars 'the Emperor', now live in the regimental museum[8] but return to the mess for the appropriate ceremonies, so that they fulfil a dual ceremonial and historic purpose. But, as the example of the history of the Buffs Regimental Museum shows, regiments could also find themselves with historic relics, trophies and mementos scattered throughout their messes and barracks, taking up space needed for other activities; it was often the imagination and enterprise of particular officers which led to these collections being brought together in an orderly fashion to form a museum (Kavanagh 1994:158).

Moreover, not all historic artifacts were originally deposited in the depot messes. Some were kept in the officers' messes which travelled with the regiments when they went to their various home and overseas postings. In those cases, as the example of the Welch Regiment demonstrates[9], some regiments, at least, were becoming aware at that time of the potential danger of loss or damage to their historic artifacts by allowing them to travel around the world, and so were willing to entrust them into the custody of the depot whether their messes were overcrowded or not.

Yet it would be unfair to suggest that these military museums were formed at this time just because of fashion or merely because some officers needed a practical solution to the overcrowding of the mess, or feared for the safety of the historic collections left with units. Indeed, a number of these museums, for example the Museum of the Devonshire Regiment[10], began by appealing for donations or loans of artifacts from private individuals or even other museums, which suggests that they may not have been bursting at the seams with their own historic objects. Others, including the King's Own Royal Regiment and the Royal Warwickshire Regiment, were worried about denuding their messes by taking away all the historic items for their new museums, and so appealed for donations or loans of more artifacts, and both the Royal Warwickshire Regiment and the Black Watch used rooms in their mess for their museums when formed.[11] In fact, in 1935 it was claimed (Cowper 1935:45) that the majority of regimental museums had less than 500 exhibits, and that included books, photographs and pictures, which suggests that they would not have imposed too much of a burden on the space available in an average officers' mess of the time. Other reasons, therefore, for the formation of these museums have to be sought.

It must be admitted that evidence for the reasons behind the establishment of military museums is not readily available, mainly because of the paucity of published or unpublished histories of these museums. There is, however, one published statement of the purpose of military museums which seems to provide some clues to this puzzle. In May 1935 Lieutenant Colonel L.I. Cowper, in an article in the *Museums Journal*, claimed that

broadly speaking the object of military museums is to keep alive the traditions of the army. They do this in three ways:-

1. By providing a storehouse of knowledge for the military historian
2. By collecting together those relics of the past which make the history of his regiment live for the recruit
3. By bringing the army and its past history to the notice of the general public

and he added that 'for the general public, the exhibits must be shown so as to make clear the importance of the army in the affairs of the nation' (Cowper 1935:40).

It is noticeable that nowhere in this list of objects of the military museum does Colonel Cowper mention a commemorative purpose.

Clearly for him these museums were predominantly for training and public relations, and to ensure that the achievements of the regiment were recorded accurately. Interestingly enough the commemorative aim for such a museum is mentioned by G.M. Bland, the civilian curator responsible for the first regimental collection to be passed to a local museum, that of the King's Own Royal Regiment in Lancaster. He claimed that the objects of such a museum were 'to lead to an intelligent understanding of the history and traditions of the regiment, to form records of notable actions and memorials to brave men, to teach recruits the history of their regiments, and to frame into a connected whole various records of the regiment', while also forming a link with the general public. It is noticeable, however, that Bland was obviously not thinking of commemorating merely the First World War, for he appealed for material to illustrate every phase of the regiment's history (*Museums Journal* 1929 28,12:399).

The first justification for the formation of museums, mentioned by both Cowper and Bland, is the desire by regiments to provide the raw material from which historians could write the history of these regiments. As has been noted, a number of regimental histories were written in the aftermath of the First World War, and not all of them simply dealt with that war. Other regiments were contemplating writing such histories in the future. The Colonel of the Welch Regiment, Major General Sir Thomas Owen Marden, for example, was preparing a history of the unit's involvement in the First World War and was concerned with the failure of the regiment to collect material relating to its history. He was also worried about the way the battalions carried around historic artifacts, and so he recommended instead the formation of a regimental museum where such material could be deposited. The decision by the Black Watch to form a small regimental museum at the depot to house 'interesting documents, books etc.' may have been stimulated by General Sir Arthur Wauchope, who was writing the Regiment's First World War history[12]. And the Dorsetshire Regiment decided in 1927 to form a museum, partly to build up a collection of articles of regimental interest which 'will assist in the compilation of a regimental History'. Their appeal seems to have been organized by the regiment's First World War historian, Colonel P.R. Phipps[13]. The year 1921 had also seen the founding of the Society for Army Historical Research which aimed to foster interest and research into the history of the British and Commonwealth land forces. It was soon publishing a quarterly *Journal* with articles on various aspects of military history, and later formed a Museum Committee which published regular bulletins on military museums.

Clearly regiments were becoming more concerned than ever before that their histories should be recorded for both internal use and public consumption for reasons which will be discussed below. It is also possible that there was some element of competition here between units. After all, Colonel G.E. Sampson, Chief Signal Officer, Aldershot, first suggested that the Royal Signals should produce a history when it was announced that the Royal Engineers were just about to publish another volume in their series of histories of their Corps and it was discovered that the Royal Canadian Corps of Signals had already produced such a history (Thwaites 1992:17). That might also explain why so many regimental museums opened up within such a short time, as each regiment strove not to be outdone by the other regiments. But it might just be that once one regiment had shown that a museum was a viable proposition others decided to take the plunge as well. Certainly the editor of the *Museums Journal* believed that the example of the King's Own Royal Regiment Museum in Lancaster inspired the formation of the East Lancashire Regiment's Museum[14] in Preston (*Museums Journal* 1934 33,8:414), and, ironically, the King's Own Royal Regiment itself noted, when discussing the formation of a museum, that 'several other units have a museum and no doubt they are of very considerable interest and historical value'[15].

As we have seen, Bland pointed out the value, as had Colonel Cowper, of the museum as a training aid for new recruits, and this was also emphasized by the Dorsetshire Regiment[16]. Until the beginning of the twentieth century the standard of recruit the army and navy were likely to receive was not high. Traditionally the other ranks of the armed services had been made up of men driven into them by hunger or the fear of a prison sentence. In line with their contemporaries they were likely to be illiterate with little formal education (Barnett 1970:343). The military authorities usually regarded these soldiers and sailors as potential criminals, drunkards and deserters who had to be kept in check by the fear of punishment. Moreover the nature of the weapons at their disposal and the perceived low intelligence of the men meant that the training they were given was on the whole simple and repetitive.

Times had changed, however, as the average recruit in the 1920s and 1930s was likely to be literate and much better educated than his nineteenth-century counterpart. Moreover, the harsh discipline of the nineteenth century was no longer socially acceptable, while at the same time technical developments and the resulting changes in tactics required a higher standard of initiative from the other ranker. The emphasis of training changed, therefore, from the blind obedience of the earlier age, based solely on parade-ground drills and repetition, to a more rounded education and more complex training. The new recruit now had to be motivated to learn, not just bullied, and the military authorities in return could expect a recruit who was more able to grasp complex ideas than his predecessor (De Watteville 1954:227–8).

It was now believed, therefore, that the new recruit could be inspired and motivated by the history and symbols of his regiment or unit in the way that only the young officers had been expected to be in the past. To achieve this, the relics, souvenirs and historic artifacts had to come out of the officers' mess and be displayed where the common soldier could see them. A museum was the most obvious place for this to happen. At the same time the soldier in training could be shown older weapons and

other equipment and illustrations of earlier battles to help him understand the way tactics had developed and what would be required of him.
It can be no coincidence that of the 50 regimental and corps museums
opened by 1935 only five were not in the regimental depot where
initial recruit training was carried out. After the Second World War
training ceased at the depots and each group of regiments had a
training battalion instead. But the military authorities recognized the
value of teaching recruits the history of their units, and so they could
still be taken to their regimental museum as an official part of their
training (Pereira 1950:23).

The third justification Colonel Cowper gives for the formation of
military museums relates to the public image of the army. The 'war to
end wars' had finished and the armed forces were shrinking fast. Yet the
regiments still had a job to do and needed to continue to attract new
recruits if they were to perform it. Their museums might help them to
accomplish this. Indeed, the editor of the *Museums Journal* hinted as
much when, reporting on the formation of the King's Own Royal
Regiment Museum, he noted that it would be housed in the public
museum of its headquarters town which 'will bring the Regiment more
closely in touch with the public from which it is mainly recruited'
(*Museums Journal* 1929 28,12:399). Significantly, as has been noted
earlier in this chapter, the majority of these new regimental museums
were already open to the public by 1935 (Cowper 1935:46–9) or aimed
to be so in time. The West Yorkshire Regiment, for example, which had
formed a museum at its York depot[17], discussed moving to another part
of the city in 1933 'where the public may have a better opportunity of
seeing the numerous relics and memorials' of the regiment (*Museums
Journal* 1934 33,7:374).

Another local regiment, the York and Lancaster Regiment, seems to
demonstrate an even closer link between the need to attract recruits
and the formation of a regimental museum. Its regimental journal, *The
Tiger and the Rose*, was, in August 1929, lamenting the fact that recruiting
had reached 'the stagnation stage', while five months later it was reporting the formation of a regimental museum at its depot in Pontefract
which, significantly perhaps, was situated in a comfortable room set
apart where '*recruits can see their friends who visit them in barracks*' (*The
Tiger and the Rose* 1930:127, my emphasis). In that way the new recruit
would be introduced to regimental history, and at the same time friends
of the right age for military service visiting them might also be
impressed by the past history and achievements of the unit[18].

Moreover, the regiments might have felt, perhaps not even con-
sciously, that it was necessary for them to show their value to the public
at a time when it was widely believed that the League of Nations
would be able to solve all international crises without resorting to
military action, and a mood of pacifism, or at least a desire for peace,
was sweeping the country. The two decades between the wars saw
the staging by the armed forces of any number of tattoos, parades and
extravaganzas to keep themselves in the public eye. It is possible that

the opening of regimental museums was in a small way a part of this public relations exercise, as Colonel Cowper seems to imply.

Yet it may also be that this wave of museum foundations simply reflects an increased pride in the history of the regiments. After all, up to the middle of the nineteenth century the armed forces, and in particular the army, had been mistrusted and despised by the general public. This had begun to change slowly during the second half of the century when the newspapers were full of the daring exploits of soldiers and sailors defending or expanding the British Empire. Moreover the Boer War, and later to an even greater extent the First World War, drew a large number of civilian volunteers into the armed forces. By 1920 the vast majority of civilians had either first-hand experience of military service or had had members of their family in the armed forces. These same armed forces had just played a major role in winning the greatest war the world had ever seen. The war may have soon lost its appeal for these civilians, but their attitude towards the armed forces could not return to what it had been before 1900. Indeed, there was often now an obvious bond of affection between the civilian population and their local regiments. This was typified in the establishment of the King's Own Royal Regiment Museum in the Lancaster City Museum in 1929. Both the City Museum's Curator, G.M. Bland, and the regiment noted the real pride which the city took in its connection with the regiment, and this was one of the main reasons why the collection was offered to the City Museum on loan, rather than being kept in the regimental barracks[19].

Whatever the reasons for their initial formation might have been, this first wave of military museum foundations stopped abruptly in 1939 on the outbreak of the Second World War. The vast majority of military museums, which after all were in military barracks, closed for the duration of the war. Their collections were put in store and their staffs turned their attention to winning the war. The national military museums also closed at the beginning of the war, though some were to reopen later (*Museums Journal* 1940 39,9:485). Organized museum activity ceased, though, of course, in the field the men and women of the armed forces and those on the Home Front were busy collecting the relics, souvenirs and trophies, carrying out the acts of bravery and winning the medals that were to form the basis of new Second World War exhibitions when the museums reopened after the war.

It was to be in many ways a very different world in which these military museums found themselves in 1945. How they coped, and are still coping, with the opportunities and challenges presented by those eventful 50 post-war years will be discussed in the next chapter.

Notes

1. A museum of the Imperial Tyrolean Jager Regiment had been formed in Austria in the early nineteenth century, and is probably Europe's first regimental museum (Cowper 1935:42).

2. *Pasley's Standing Orders (1818), Section XIV The Model Rooms.* The material in this section on the Royal Engineers Museum is based on extracts from various sources kindly sent to me by Andrew Gladwell, the Assistant Curator of the Royal Engineers Museum.

3. See for example 'Birmingham's War Memorial scheme abandoned . . . in view of the strong feeling entertained by many citizens that a war museum . . . would not constitute an adequate memorial of the men who had laid down their lives for the country' (*Museums Journal* 1919 18,7:186).

4. For example, by August 1918, even before the war was over, the Canadian Army Medical Corps had put together a collection of wax and plaster models, drawings, and photographs of wounds which were on display in the Royal College of Surgeons (*Museums Journal*, 1918 18,4:74). Moreover, John Buchan, the famous author and later Head of the Department of Information, had suggested in 1915 that every regiment should have its own official historian (Kavanagh 1994: 120).

5. This collection is now in the Prince of Wales's Own Regiment of Yorkshire Museum.

6. As early as 1920 it had been proposed that Edinburgh Castle should be the site of the Scottish War Memorial, with the military hospital at the entrance used for housing the trophies of Scottish regiments, and the eighteenth-century barracks turned into a museum (*Museums Journal*, 1920 19,9:20).

7. The King's Own Royal Regiment Museum, for example, began with over 1000 items which covered the whole history of the regiment from its formation in 1680 (*Museums Journal*, 1930 29,8:287), and the Regimental Museum of the Cameronians was appealing for material prior to 1860, soon after its foundation (*Museums Journal*, 1933 33,1:97).

8. 'The Emperor' is held in the Lancashire County and Regimental Museum.

9. The Welch Regiment historian, Major General Sir Thomas Owen Marden, was worried about the possible loss of the historic artifacts which were being taken by the battalions of the regiment to their various postings. He quoted the example of the fire which occurred in the 1st Battalion's Officers' Mess in Pembroke Dock in 1895 and destroyed historic artifacts as well as regimental silver. Letter from Lieutenant B. Owen, RN (Retd), FMA, Curator of the Welch Regiment Museum, to the author, 1 November 1994.

10. This collection now forms part of the Military Museum of Devon and Dorset.

11. Letter from P. Donnelly, Assistant Keeper, Museum of the King's Own Royal Regiment, to the author, 1 November 1994, including extracts from the regimental journal *The Lion and the Rose*; letter from Brigadier J.K. Chater, Regimental Area Secretary (Warwickshire), the Royal Regiment of Fusiliers, to the author, 2 November 1994, including extracts from the regimental journal *The Antelope*; letter from Major (Retd) A.R. McKinnell, MBE, Curator, The Black Watch Museum, to the author, drawing on various editions of the regimental journal *The Red Hackle*, 1 November 1994.

12. Letter from Major McKinnell to the author, *op. cit.*

13. Letter from Major J. Carroll, Curator of the Military Museum of Devon and Dorset to the author, 9 November 1994.

14. This is now in the Blackburn Museum and Art Gallery.

15. *The Lion and the Rose*, January 1928, p.5.

16. Letter from Major J. Carroll, *op. cit.*

17. This collection is also in the Prince of Wales's Own Regiment of Yorkshire Museum.

18. This connection was drawn to my attention by D.W. Scott, Keeper (Militaria), Rotherham Department of Libraries, Museum and Arts, in a letter to the author, 21 November 1994.

19. *The Lion and the Rose* of January 1928, and G.M. Bland, quoted in the May 1929 edition. The regiment was also aware, however, as the January 1928 article makes clear, of the advantages, in terms of visitor numbers, to be gained by having its collection in the central city museum rather than in the confines of the barracks.

3. The Development of Military Museums

In terms of educating tomorrow's citizens, keeping the services in the public eye and improving public understanding of their role and importance, the (military) museums are part of the fabric of the services; not a desirable extra, but a quintessential part.

(Museums and Galleries Commission 1990:42)

There was no call during the Second World War for the formation of local war museums. That battle had been fought and lost in the war-weariness of 1918. But the Second World War was the People's War, where the contribution to the final victory made by ordinary men and women was even more clearly recognized, by both the government and the people themselves, than it had been a generation before. As a result, it would be a rare local history museum which did not have its Home Front, Home Guard and ARP displays after the war. The main military museum structure was, of course, already in place and could easily adjust to the new war. The Imperial War Museum had its terms of reference extended to cover this conflict and the regimental and corps museums, when they reopened, just added more artifacts and enlarged their medal displays.

The next 15 years saw mixed fortunes for the regimental and corps museums. On the one hand, many of those that had been formed before the war were able to reopen in 1945, and every year more and more new ones were founded in line with the general boom in new museums at this time[1]. Moreover, National Service, which lasted until 1962, meant a regular intake of new recruits who had to be trained and inculcated with pride in their regiment or corps, and this guaranteed that the work of the regimental and corps museums would continue to seem worthwhile.

On the other hand, money was initially scarce in the harsh post-war conditions. Regiments did not have the funds to pay for the construction of purpose-built museums and so had to rely on misemploying other space. But many units found it hard to set aside space for their museum, as the need to accommodate and train so many National Service recruits put pressure on the available barrack rooms. The Royal Signals Museum, for example, had officially been established in 1938, but no suitable accommodation had been found for its collection before the outbreak of war in 1939, so objects spent the war years in store. It was hoped that the end of the war and the expansion of Catterick Camp, in which the museum was sited, would enable a suitable building to be provided. But space remained at a premium in the camp, and it was not until 1953 that a hut could be set aside in which to display the collection (Thwaites 1992:19). Similar problems afflicted the Welch Regiment Museum and the Duke of Cornwall's Light Infantry Regimental Museum, amongst others[2]. Even those museums, like the Worcestershire Regimental Museum, which had allocated a room in which to set out their collections, might be forced to move, if an official use was found for the accommodation that they inhabited (Pereira 1948:55).

The problem was that, unlike the national military museums (the Imperial War Museum, which was initially funded via the Ministry of Education, and the Scottish United Services Museum, which originally came under the Ministry of Public Buildings and Works), no official funding had been made available to the regimental and corps museums. It was true that a blind eye had usually been turned to their use of barrack accommodation for their unofficial museums, and units had even been allowed, since the 1940s, to maintain a soldier on depot strength to keep the museum clean (Pereira 1950:236). But, in general, regiments had no entitlement to a museum, and that meant that no War Office money was forthcoming to pay for the construction and maintenance of the displays, for the purchase of artifacts or for the employment of staff. What money regimental and corps museums did receive generally came either from regimental funds and donations from old comrades, or as a result of public appeals (Cowper 1935:43–4).

As we have seen, accommodation could often be obtained by re-allocating barrack rooms, or by using rooms in the mess, while display cases might be built using the unit's workshops. But staffing was a bigger problem. A cleaner might be found from amongst the soldiers on the strength awaiting a posting, or, as in the case of the Royal Signals Museum, a part-time cleaner could be paid from unit funds (Thwaites 1992:19), but a curator was needed and would cost much more than a cleaner to employ. Therefore, as no government money was available to pay for a full-time curator, and most units could not afford this expense, the job was undertaken on an unofficial basis by the Regimental Secretary or some other officer on the Depot staff who, with no formal training or previous experience, tried to combine his museum post with all his other regimental duties. Alternatively the post would be given to a retired member of the regiment, usually an officer who had some interest in military history, who, because he was already in receipt of an army pension, was able to take on the job either unpaid, or at the pittance that the regiment could afford. It is not surprising that military museums often had displays, labels, storage methods and finding aids which gave professional civilian curators much cause for concern; nor that many of them remained pitifully small organizations, housed in inadequate and unsuitable buildings, and lacking the most basic visitor facilities.

This totally unsatisfactory position was rectified to some extent at least when, in June 1956, the War Office issued Army Council Instruction 282. This acknowledged that 'As there is no Army Museum, the military museums organised by regiments and corps comprise primarily the repositories for the care and preservation of military relics ... they are the custodians of the military heirlooms of our country' (quoted in *Museums Journal* 1957 57,7:196). It continued by authorizing the employment of a museum orderly, acting as attendant and general handyman, the provision of furniture and fittings and heating and lighting at public expense, and the use of some basic accommodation to a fixed scale (Moss 1970:1). But more importantly it acknowledged the War Office's official involvement in the provision of military museums (which was inherited and continued by the MoD), though it did not, as Colonel Cowper (1935:44) had suggested in 1935 that it should, establish a policy for the museums it supported.

War Office involvement had been growing slowly since the end of the Second World War. It had set up in the aftermath of that war a Military Museums Co-ordinating Committee comprising representatives of the Royal Armouries, the Royal United Service Institution Museum, the Royal Military Academy Sandhurst Museum, the Royal Artillery Institution, The Castle Museum, York, and the Society for Army Historical Research, chaired by the Director of Weapons and Development. Its primary function seems to have been similar to that of the Committee on Military Museums, first set up in 1913 (Lewis 1992b:33), which was to ensure a fair and logical distribution of major military artifacts. But it could also give advice to regimental and corps museums.

In 1952 it attempted to bring the smaller regimental and corps museums into the mainstream of the museum world by suggesting the setting up of a Federation of Military Museums under its auspices, which would be affiliated to the Museums Association. It hoped that this Federation would act as a forum in which military museums would be able to help each other and perhaps gain professional advice from their civilian counterparts in the Museums Association[3]. This body was never a great success, and when sponsorship of regimental and corps museums was taken over in 1966 by PS(12), the branch of the Ministry of Defence responsible for ceremonial and public display matters, it began a series of periodic conferences of military curators within each Army Command. These have acted ever since as the main forum for the exchange of information, advice and help between the museums (Moss 1970:22).

An even more important event was the foundation of the Army Museums Ogilby Trust, which took place in 1954. This trust was set up by Colonel R.J.L. Ogilby, Joint Honorary Colonel of the 1st Battalion of the London Scottish (TA) Regiment, who provided the sum of £100,000 to form the nucleus of its fund. The Trust was established 'to promote and foster regimental and military tradition primarily by the encouragement, equipment, care and maintenance of existing regimental and army museums and the establishment of additional museums' (*Museums Journal* 1955 54,12:331). Its long-term aim was the establishment of a central national army museum, which was finally realized in 1971.

The Trust has over the last 40 years provided small sums to enable military museums to purchase suitable objects for their collections and to make other improvements. This has enabled Territorial Army museums in particular, which have no official status, to obtain the small sums of money they need to carry on acquiring and displaying their collections (Newton 1987b:150). But the Trust acts now mainly as a centre for research and information on all aspects of military collections, as a source of advice for military curators and as a pressure group on behalf of military museums and museums with military collections. It has always had the approval of the Army Board of the Defence Council[4] and of the civilian museum bodies.

Perhaps, though, its greatest achievement has been to persuade regiments to set up museum trusts to ensure the security of regimental collections. Before signing these trust documents, some regiments tended to use their museums as stores from which historic uniforms and other artifacts could be drawn for use in parades, tattoos or demonstrations, to the detriment of these items. Moreover, the objects had no long-term protection and could be sold, swapped or destroyed as the regiment saw fit. Under the terms of the trust, however, conditions are laid down as to when, to whom and for what purpose objects can be loaned, along with regulations governing the disposal of single objects or collections. These documents have, therefore, taken the museum collections out of the category of disposable regimental property in which they had previously resided. In that way the collections of disbanded units have been given long-term protection because, under the terms of the trust, if a museum closes and no new home can be found for the collection, it automatically passes to the care of the National Army Museum.

In most cases, of course, regimental collections were not in any danger from thoughtless or greedy members of the regiment, because the historical worth of these artifacts was fully appreciated. But these trusts have also meant the establishment of trustee bodies, often a mixture of serving and retired members of the regiment or corps, who are responsible for the museum and its collection, set policy for it, raise money, act as its champions and generally advance its cause. These museums no longer have to rely for their continued well-being, therefore, on the initiative, effort and enthusiasm of particular individual officers, as they often did in their early years (see Kavanagh 1994:158).

By 1960, then, military museums had grown in number, had been given official status, some staffing and official accommodation, and their collections had acquired legal protection. The next decade even offered the possibility of a large increase in numbers, as the cavalry regiments began to open their own museums. As was noted in the Introduction, since 1881 definite and stable territorial areas had been allocated to infantry regiments from which they could draw their recruits. They had set up their depots in those areas, and these in turn had become the homes of their museums, though some regimental collections had found a more suitable home in the relevant local museum. Corps did not usually have this strong local connection, but they still had a central depot or training centre which could act as their focus, and, later, the site of their museum. Cavalry regiments, on the other hand, had been supplied with recruits from central depots and had no home bases as such. They had been forced to carry their possessions, including their historic collections, with them wherever they were posted. The situation was alleviated somewhat in 1954 when space was provided at the Royal Military Academy Museum at Sandhurst to house historic cavalry objects. This museum had been set up in 1949 'to preserve those objects of interest in connection with the army which do not fall readily within the scope of existing establishments' (Boultbee 1951:16). Space had already been found there for the collections of disbanded Irish regiments and for Indian Army relics (Pereira 1950:235), and so it seemed an appropriate repository for these cavalry artifacts (Moss 1970:5).

But the real solution to their problem came in the early 1960s when Home Headquarters were authorized for the cavalry regiments under a Defence Council Instruction which also granted them permission to form their own museums. This enabled the Queen's Own Hussars, for example, whose Home Headquarters was in Warwick, to set up a museum in the Chaplain's Dining Hall of Lord Leycesters Hospital in 1964, and the Queen's Dragoon Guards to establish their museum, with the help of the local borough council, in Clive's House, Shrewsbury, in 1968. Today the majority of the cavalry museums are managed within local authority museums (MGC 1990:23).

But the late 1950s and early 1960s also heralded a time of change and reorganization for the armed forces, which had dramatic effects on many military museums (Moss 1970:3). Faced with financial stringencies and a parallel shrinking of Britain's role in international affairs, a policy of rationalizing the armed forces was begun in those years which has not finished yet. Major Defence Reviews were carried out in 1957, 1965, 1974, and 1981, and between 1991 and 1994. At each stage substantial cuts have been made in men or equipment, or both. For example, National Service was finally ended in 1962, and the strength of the army was cut by half in five years. As a result, 45 infantry regiments had been disbanded, amalgamated or placed in suspended animation by 1969; 2 more amalgamated in 1970 and 3 were disbanded in 1971.

The formation of new regiments from these amalgamations had obvious implications for their museums. The formation in 1966 of the Queen's Regiment can act as an example of these changes. In 1959 the Queen's Royal Regiment (West Surreys) amalgamated with the East Surrey Regiment to form the Queen's Royal Surrey Regiment. The West Surrey Regiment's collection from Guildford was added to the East Surrey Regiment's Museum at Kingston, Surrey, to form a new joint museum, which is now at Claydon Park near Guildford. In 1961 the Buffs (the Royal East Kent Regiment) amalgamated with the Queen's Own Royal West Kents to form The Queen's Own Buffs (The Royal Kent Regiment). The West Kents' Depot in Maidstone was closed and its museum moved into the Maidstone Museum. Finally, in 1966 the

Queen's Own Buffs amalgamated with the Queen's Royal Surrey
Regiment, the Royal Sussex Regiment and the Middlesex Regiment
to form the Queen's Regiment. The new regiment formed its own
museum in Canterbury (which later moved to Dover Castle). Meanwhile the Buffs Regimental Museum moved into a branch museum
of the City of Canterbury, the Middlesex Regiment Museum was
established at Bruce Castle, the TA centre in Edgware (this museum has
since closed and the collection is now held in the National Army
Museum), and the Royal Sussex Regiment's collection was transferred
to the Chichester City Museum (Moss 1970:3), but is now in the Sussex
Combined Services Museum.

From this example it can be seen that no clear pattern emerged. Some
regimental museums survived intact with enlarged collections, though
rarely with greater space. Moreover, by remaining within military
barracks, they were unwittingly storing up trouble for themselves for,
in the 1980s, increased IRA activity meant the imposition of greater
security measures on camps, which acted as a disincentive to visitors
(MGC 1990:24). Others found new accommodation, in private premises
or in other official buildings, though their existence, if they had no living
regiment to support them, was often not an enviable one. That was
unless they became one of those military museums set up in castles,
which, like the 1st The Queen's Dragoon Guards Regimental Museum
in Cardiff Castle (Figure 3.1) and the Regimental Museum of the Argyll
and Sutherland Highlanders in Stirling Castle, enjoy the undoubted
benefits in terms of visitor numbers of being sited in a major tourist
attraction. Other regiments passed their collections on permanent loan
to the relevant local authority museum service, often with a financial
settlement from the MoD to help set up the new museum or gallery, and
perhaps with some contribution to running costs in the short term at
least (MGC 1990:34).

Under this latter arrangement a number of notable military museums
have been formed, but this was not, of course, a new solution. The first
collection to be passed on loan to a local authority for display was that
of the King's Own Royal Regiment, which was placed in the Lancaster
City Museum in 1929, even before most regimental museums had been
formed. By the 1960s, though, regimental museum trustees were
said to be increasingly willing to accept this solution because of 'the
feeling of insecurity resulting from continuous army reorganisation',
and regimental authorities were 'desirous of housing their museums
in such a way as to be no longer subject to MoD changes of policy' (Moss
1970:15).

But in some cases this solution has not turned out to be an ideal one.
Even though councils may have been willing to accept the collections
because of the strong local connection between the regiment and the
town or county, that has not always meant that the collections have
been appreciated or understood by the local museum service (MGC
1990:35–6). Some have been largely relegated to the store (Thorburn
1962:189 and Moss 1970:24), while others, like the Royal Warwickshire

Figure 3.1 Interior of the 1st The Queen's Dragoon Guards Regimental Museum. The displays have been fitted into the shape of the walls of Cardiff Castle.

Source: 1st The Queen's Dragoon Guards Regimental Museum

Regimental Museum, have been granted accommodation by their local authority but no funding, leaving them in the unenviable position of trying to raise all the finance they need for any new acquisitions or new capital developments by public appeals. Even the flagship of these accommodations, the Durham Light Infantry Museum scheme, has been criticized in the past because it was claimed (Moss 1970:19) that the local authority was only really interested in the art gallery, which is collocated with the Durham Light Infantry collection, and had shown no further concern for the military museum.

It should be emphasized, however, that many military collections would have disappeared without trace during those difficult years if it were not for the intervention of local councils, and many of those in local authority care now have the advantage of being looked after, for the first time in their history, by professional curators and conservators. Moreover, both the MoD and some of the keenest supporters of military museums see absorption into the relevant local authority museum service as the only viable future for most regular regiment museums (Newton 1987a:67) and for their volunteer regiment counterparts (Rivis 1957:198).

At the same time the Ministry of Defence continued to support some of the museums (and Regimental Headquarters (RHQs)) of regiments that had amalgamated, if the local authority could not be persuaded to take them over, partly as a way of maintaining links with the traditional recruiting areas of the constituent units. For example, on the amalgamation of the Duke of Cornwall's Light Infantry with the Somerset Light Infantry, both constituent regiments were allowed to retain their RHQs and museums in their traditional recruiting areas. As a result of this policy, by 1990 there were still approximately 160 regimental and corps museums at 140 sites, only 40 of which were managed within local museum services.

For the 100 or so museums that the MoD supported directly, it issued a Defence Council Instruction (109) in 1966 which laid down the authorized size and staffing of its museums. For infantry brigade depots, those housing three regiments could have an area of 1500 square feet, while four regiment depots could add an extra 300 square feet. In the case of single regimental headquarters, the allowance was 750 square feet and a store of 200 square feet for non-amalgamated regiments, and twice that for amalgamated ones. If such regiments had a split RHQ (i.e. one in each of the original sites of the two regiments) then the total allowance was split between them. No size was specified for the Royal Artillery Regiment or the corps museums, but they had to obtain MoD approval for their buildings. This allowance might not seem generous and, of course, it did not mean that the MoD would pay for new purpose-built museums of these dimensions: it merely authorized the use of existing MoD property up to these sizes. But fittings and furniture, as had been stated in 1956, were to be provided at public expense, as were fuel, light, telephone and the general maintenance costs of the building.

The allowance for staffing was similarly specified: normally one attendant for most small museums, with perhaps the addition of a full-time curator for the larger museums, though, in fact, there has always been some variation on this basic allocation, particularly for the larger museums[5]. But unfortunately the majority of MoD museums were still expected to rely on the services of the Regimental Secretary or some other member of the staff at RHQ to act as part-time, untrained curator (augmented in practice by equally untrained volunteers and full and part-time ancillary staff paid for out of regimental funds), even though the Defence Council Instruction insisted that 'every facility should be provided for the inspection of the museum by the general public', and continued that 'It is desirable that the admittance hours of the museum should include if possible week-ends and early closing days'. Moreover, the range of duties expected of the curator, as laid down in the Army General and Administrative Instruction (AGAI) 115, which formalized MoD support for its museums, suggested that they could only be achieved by a full-time post holder (MGC 1990:28). Perhaps it is not surprising that the MGC Working Party, visiting these regimental and corps museums over 30 years after the MoD had begun to give them some official support, still found that (MGC 1990:38) 'standards of collections care commonly leave something to be desired, and in some cases are extremely poor'.

Yet at the same time the MoD was making a major contribution towards the foundation of military museums in this country. In 1960 collections began to accumulate at the museum in Sandhurst which were to form the basis of the National Army Museum (NAM). Its Royal Charter, signed by the Queen on 5 May 1960, states that its functions are to collect, preserve and exhibit objects and records relating to the history of the Army and by so doing to make better known the Army's achievements, history and traditions. From relatively small beginnings, the Museum's collections grew rapidly, and, through the efforts of Field Marshal Sir Gerald Templer, AMOT, and others, sufficient funds were raised to construct a larger, purpose-built museum on a site in Chelsea. The new building was opened in November 1971. The MoD had not paid for the building, but did subsequently pay for its upkeep and for the staffing of this national museum, as well as providing its operating funds.

Two years later the MoD provided the buildings, the staff and operating funds to bring together the Victory Museum and the McCarthy Collection of Nelson material to form the Royal Naval Museum at Portsmouth. Both of these developments will be discussed in more detail in Chapter 9.

The 1960s and 1970s were in fact another period of growth in the provision of military museums. In addition to the formation of NAM and the Royal Naval Museum, the Fleet Air Arm Museum was opened in Yeovilton in 1964 and expanded greatly in the next decade, as did the Tank Museum at Bovington and the RAF Museum at Hendon, while the Imperial War Museum grew dramatically in the same period by taking over the ex-RAF station at Duxford to house and display its aircraft and vehicle collections. This period also saw the formation of one of the few non-national tri-service museums, when the Eastbourne Borough Council established a museum illustrating the history of the military forces in the Sussex area (*Museums Bulletin* 1978 18:12).

Then in 1976 a small working party was set up in the MoD to conduct a survey of regimental museums and to see how it could assist its museums more, while at the same time obtaining benefits in return in the field of education, recruiting and public relations[6]. No dramatic changes occurred as a result of its work, though the survey demonstrated that the MoD was aware of its relationship with these museums. Moreover, while regimental and corps museums had originally been authorized to fulfil a heritage and public relations role in the absence of a national army museum, the subsequent opening of NAM had not resulted in the MoD withdrawing its support from them. The AGAI 115.002 authorizing museums was amended to state that 'the primary role of regimental and corps museums is to collect and preserve regimental and corps relics and make them accessible to the regiment and corps and to the general public, thereby fostering an interest in the past, present and future of the regiment or corps, and also providing an educational facility for the public' (quoted in MGC 1990:22).

The MoD was still aware, however, of a need to control its spending on non-essential activities. It sees its primary task, quite rightly, as maintaining national defence, and anything which does not seem to increase its capability to do this will be first on the block when the financial axe is wielded, and, as Stephen Wood (1986a:14) has noted, 'regimental museums for all their charm do not kill Russians'. In 1980, therefore, as part of a review of its policy towards Infantry RHQs, the Army Board asked Colonel J.R. Billington to prepare a report on army museums. He was tasked with establishing the present cost to the MoD of maintaining regimental and corps museums and with making recommendations concerning both a long-term policy for achieving savings in manpower, accommodation and running costs, and the measures that should be taken towards the rationalization of the present museums and their assimilation, where possible, into civic museums (MGC 1990:30).

This latter point was considered particularly important, as one of the main expenses of these museums to the Defence Vote was the cost of their occupation of MoD accommodation, though it was conceded that some museums would not be able to find a suitable civilian museum, castle or stately home willing to accept their collection.

After it had received the Billington Report, the Army Board re-affirmed its view that the regimental and corps museums played a vital role by contributing to morale within the army by helping to create a favourable image of the army in the public mind and thereby providing 'an important, if unquantifiable, aid to recruiting' (MGC 1990:31). It promised to maintain MoD support for existing authorized museums, but would not guarantee any increase in provision, and said it should continue to encourage arrangements with local museums. At the same time it announced two new policy decisions. The first stated that it would cease to support financially any museum which received less than 5000 visitors a year, while the second was that, where possible, museums should institute entrance charges from which the MoD would receive some pay-back. Both these policies were subsequently honoured more in the breach than in the observance, but they suggested that the MoD was now clearly thinking of the cost of running these museums, and of ways of reducing this burden as much as possible (MGC 1990:31).

Apart, however, from the need to produce a regular return on visitor numbers, most military museums noticed little change as a result of the Billington Report. But the 1980s none the less proved to be a period of considerable change for many of them. This was a boom time for museums. New ones were opening at a remarkable rate, and the new breed of independent museums seemed to be showing the way forward, with modern display design, improved visitor facilities and a more commercial approach to their operations. But military museums, on the whole, appeared to be lagging behind. In 1981 Lieutenant Colonel (Retd) George Forty took over as Director and Curator of the Tank Museum and found a situation which he claims (Forty 1987:73) was common to many military museums. His museum was short of money, understaffed and deficient in covered exhibition area and all but the basic visitor amenities, and suffered from a lack of purpose beyond catering for the small number of experts who visited the museum. He and his contemporaries at the Fleet Air Arm Museum and the Museum of Army Flying knew that their museums had to grow and develop, and saw that the paucity of support available from the MoD need not limit this growth. They turned instead to the introduction of entrance charges, improved shop and catering operations, fundraising and commercial sponsorship to provide the financial resources they needed to help them build new galleries, to improve their displays and their facilities and to increase their staff numbers, in order to make their museums more efficient and more attractive to the general public (Forty 1987:73). They became, therefore, more like the independent museums. For those museums less able to be commercially independent, though, the funds made available by the MoD, in the face of continuing Treasury pressure to control non-essential spending, seemed increasingly inadequate in the context of the vastly higher standards of management and presentation now being used in other museums (MGC 1990:27).

At the same time, more interest than ever before was being shown in the philosophy and purpose of these museums. In October 1983 Kenneth Hudson published an article (Hudson 1983) in which he reviewed some of the developments that had taken place in military museums in the past 20 years. He praised the increased professionalism of most of them, but suggested that some rationalization and regrouping would have to take place in the near future to ease the burden on the MoD, while at the same time making military museums more viable. Then, in the period 1986–7, Stephen Wood (1986a, 1986b, 1987a, 1987b), the Keeper of the Scottish United Services Museum, carried on a seemingly one-sided debate in the columns of the leading museum publications. He criticized the old-fashioned, object-based, esoteric displays of traditional military museums, and argued that they needed to make their subject more accessible and more relevant to people's lives.

Even as he was writing these articles a number of military museum developments were echoing his words. In April 1987 the new Museum of the Manchesters was opened in Ashton-under-Lyne. In it the collection of the now defunct Manchester Regiment was shown within the context of the social history of the Manchester people who lived around its barracks and from whom it obtained its recruits. At the same time the National Army Museum was planning the complete refurbishment of its galleries, starting with an exhibition called 'The Road To Waterloo', in which the story of the military campaign was interspersed with displays which showed the daily life of the soldiers and their camp followers. In 1990 the new Gurkha Museum went a stage further, setting the story of these Nepalese soldiers within the framework of their civilian lives; it also showed how the agricultural and domestic work of their women allowed these men to turn to soldiering. The newly refurbished Regiments of Gloucestershire Museum, opened in the same year, focused on the realities of life for the soldier and his dependents (Beresford 1991:27).

These and similar developments seemed to indicate that at least some
military museums were coming out of the darkness of the specialized,
'family' museum and emerging into the light as more commercialized,
but also more generally appealing, members of the community of social
history museums to which Stephen Wood and others had long suggested
that they belonged. Nevertheless, the MGC Working Party Report,
The Museums of the Armed Services, published in 1990, noted that 'too many
museums, despite paying lip service to the need to attract and educate
the general public, are still aiming their displays primarily at the
regimental or corps "family", and at the military historian' (MGC
1990:39).

Moreover, the same report was to show that all was not well in the
management of these military museums. This review, undertaken by
Admiral Sir David Williams, exposed a number of anomalies in the way
in which the MoD dealt with its military museums. The report noted
that, while it did a great deal for the 100 or so museums it sustained,
the MoD had no consistent policy towards them. Some, like the naval
museums, were encouraged to develop and to become more commercial by being allowed to keep the money they raised. On the other hand,
the army museums were less likely to get support for their development
plans and would be expected to return to the MoD a portion of any
money they raised. In general the Report (MGC 1990:39) argued
that 'Museums need to be assured of adequate funding to cover a
reasonable proportion of their running costs', and urged the MoD 'to
maintain at least its present levels of support in real terms'. It also
suggested that 'the MoD centrally should accept the need to adopt a
consistent policy towards museums, decide what coordinating machinery
is needed to achieve this, and put it in place as soon as practicable',
echoing what Colonel Cowper (1935:45) had argued 55 years before.

The MoD responded to this critical report by commissioning two
reports of its own, neither of which have so far been made public. The
first was to consider whether the MoD wanted to keep the national
museums it controlled, and, if so, how it was to manage them effectively
and efficiently. The second was to study the future needs of the regimental and corps museums directly or indirectly funded by the MoD,
and to consider the points made by the MGC report in relation to these
museums to see which of its recommendations should be implemented
(*AIM Bulletin* 1991 14:2). At the same time Brigadier C.L.G. Henshaw,
who was preparing the latter report with the assistance of Colonel Peter
Walton of AMOT, was to see what savings could be made in the cost of
this museum provision. Brigadier Henshaw seems to have been generally
supportive of regimental and corps museums, concluding that they
still had an important service function, though he argued that these
museums, to be effective, needed to update their displays and to show a
greater awareness of the social history context within which the history
of the regiments and the lives of the soldiers should be shown. His main
suggestions on savings involved the closure or amalgamation of museums
that represented defunct regiments and the greater encouragement of

the absorption of regimental museums within the local museum service whenever possible. He urged that the funding and management of these museums should be undertaken centrally, with standardized management systems and performance measures (*AIM Bulletin* 1991 14:6).

In fact, regimental museum mergers and local authority museum service takeovers of the kind he had apparently recommended were already taking place. A new joint venture between the local authorities, the regimental and corps museums' trustees and the MoD was announced in 1990 to bring together a number of military museums into a new museum and 'military experience' complex in Aldershot. Meanwhile the museums of the Royal Hussars, the Royal Green Jackets, the Light Infantry and the Gurkhas had moved into two refurbished barrack blocks in Winchester, supported in part by the local authority, and a project was being considered in Hamilton to merge the Cameronians Regimental Museum with the Hamilton District Museum (Boardman 1990:14). Meanwhile, the Royal Naval Museum was attempting to move into a closer relationship with the other attractions in the Portsmouth Naval Heritage area (Thomas 1994:16). But the Devons and Dorsets Regiment, which was to lose MoD support for one of its museums, decided to concentrate its two collections in the Keep at Dorchester, as the Military Museum of Devon and Dorset, and to retain its presence in Devon through small displays at four sites.

But, even before Brigadier Henshaw had begun his review, a new political development arose which was eventually to throw everything back into the melting pot. In November 1989 the Berlin Wall was finally torn down, heralding the collapse of the Eastern Bloc. Within a dramatically short time the Cold War seemed to be over and the main military threat to this country had disappeared. Politicians now wanted a peace dividend that they could pass on to their voters. The most obvious benefit from this outbreak of peace would be the possibility of a drastic reduction of the armed forces. In July 1990 the Secretary of State for Defence announced the setting up of a study, under the title 'Options for Change', which would look into the future size and structure of Britain's armed forces. The results of the study were announced in July 1991. The main recommendations were that, in addition to the cancellation of several new weapons developments and the cutting back of both the number of ships in the Royal Navy and the number of air-craft in the RAF, the army was to suffer 15 regimental mergers and a reduction in the number of personnel in the corps. The planned changes also envisaged the concentration of training functions in fewer sites with a subsequent closure of a number of army camps.

Several of the parts of the plan had implications for military museums. The amalgamations would leave another group of museums without a sponsoring unit, and the closure of camps would make some museums homeless (Greene 1991:13). A further blow came with the MoD's decision to cut its civilian staff complement by 30 per cent and its overall budget by the same amount to meet Treasury targets. This made Henshaw's Report, when it appeared in February 1992, seem suddenly over-generous and over-optimistic, and the savings he suggested inadequate.

In April 1993 the Adjutant General took over the funding of RHQs and regimental museums. The Director General Adjutant General's Corps was tasked with establishing a policy for these RHQs and museums which would include firm proposals for achieving the 30 per cent savings demanded by the Treasury. As a result a further report was produced which made recommendations on how the 30 per cent savings for the 1995/96 budget could be achieved. These cuts were said by Clare Conybeare (1994:9) to threaten the funding of 60 regimental museums, though Colonel Mary Rook, the head of the Regimental Headquarters and Museums Department in the Headquarters of the Director General Adjutant General's Corps, argued that the proposed cuts 'may have no appreciable impact as the MoD's contribution to museums is very modest', while admitting that it was too early to be certain (quoted in Conybeare 1994:9). Colonel Peter Walton, Secretary of AMOT, contended that the MoD was the victim of Treasury inter-ference, and complained that 'it is unfortunate in the extreme that the MoD has been unable to develop a comprehensive policy for the management of its museums and their contribution to the army and to the wider community' (quoted in Conybeare 1994:9).

Just, therefore, at a time when the standards of military museums were beginning to rise, partly as a result of the prompting of the MoD, the department responsible for their funding was having to make financial savings which might make any further improvements much harder to achieve, and could even endanger the future of some of these museums. Moreover, it had apparently still failed to establish a clear policy for them. Indeed doubts were beginning to be expressed about the appropriateness of the MoD supporting museums. A cross-party committee of the House of Commons reported in 1994 (quoted in *AIM Bulletin* 1994,17:5) on the current status of these museums and argued that 'it was inappropriate for the Ministry of Defence to be in charge of museums. Their expenditure plans for the period up to 1996 contained no reference at all to its museums. The RAF Museum fund-ing arrangements, for instance, were deplorable. The role of the MoD lay in the defence of the country, not as curator'. It concluded that 'responsibility for all aspects of heritage ought to be with the DNH (Department of National Heritage), and funding for MoD museums should be transferred to this Department'. The MoD apparently does not agree. It also seems to have decided that its museums would not have to endure the 30 per cent cutbacks after all, though Colonel Peter Walton, Secretary of AMOT (quoted in *AIM Bulletin* 1994,17:3), warned that this may only be a temporary respite.

Meanwhile, interest in military museums within the museum profession was, if anything, increasing. In 1990 one of the debates at the Museums Association Annual Conference was concerned with the best way of portraying military history in museums, while a WHAM conference on Women and Weapons considered how women could be written back into the galleries containing military artifacts, so as to attract them as well as the male enthusiast. And the public did not show any appreciable lessening in their interest in these museums, though, like their civilian counterparts, military museums suffered some fall in visitor figures during the recession.

As we shall see in Chapter 10, moreover, the uncertainty surrounding the future funding of these museums has not prevented a fresh wave of redevelopments. Indeed, if anything it has encouraged military museums to speed up the modernization of their displays and customer facilities. Some museum trustees, like, for example, those of the Royal Artillery museums and of the Royal Signals Museum, have accepted that, if future support from the MoD is uncertain, they can only ensure the viability of their museums by attracting more paying visitors. To do this, they have to provide more exciting and relevant exhibitions and better customer care, even if that entails launching public appeals to raise the funds needed to build larger, more modern museums with improved facilities and displays.

Local-authority-funded military museums are not immune from this financial threat. The current local government reorganization has cast doubt on the future funding of some local authority museums, and government instructions to local authorities to keep down spending on non-essential local services is also putting pressure on museum services. Trustees of some of the military museums within local authority museum services, like those of the Royal Warwickshire Regimental Museum and of the King's Own Royal Regiment Museum, are also reacting positively by attempting to raise the funds needed to improve their displays and thereby attract more visitors. For free-entry local authority museums this will not result in more money through the door, but it will demonstrate the important part that these museums can play in the local museum provision.

As Chapter 10 will show, some positive developments have come out of the recession of the 1990s, and the future for military museums is not all gloomy, though some still have some way to go before they can be confident about their future viability.

I have given the historical background to these regimental collections and their museums in so much detail because I believe it helps to explain the way in which military history has been displayed in the past, and why these displays have been forced to change in the last two decades and may continue to develop in the near future. In the next chapter I shall examine in more detail how warfare, which for perhaps 70 years was considered the most important aspect of the military history depicted in military museums, is dealt with in their displays.

Notes

1. 'There has been a terrific growth in the number of museums in Britain since the Second World War. From somewhere in the region of 700 museums, there

are now over 2000' (Kavanagh 1993:19). Ken Barton (1980) claimed that 30 new regimental museums opened between 1945 and 1980.

2. Letter from Lieutenant B. Owen, RN(Retd), FMA, Curator, the Welch Regiment Museum, to the author, 1 November 1994; and letter from Major (Retd) W.H. White DL, Curator of the Duke of Cornwall's Light Infantry Regimental Museum, to the author, 2 November 1994.

3. See *Museums Journal,* (1953), 53,3:87, and Major M.H.D. Lord, (quoted in *Museums Journal,* (1953), 53, 5:134).

4. It is listed as a source of advice in Army General and Administrative Instructions (AGAI) 115, the document which defines the MoD's support for military museums. Before AMOT was formed, military museum curators could gain advice from the Museum Committee of the Society for Army Historical Research (*Museums Journal,* (1957), 57, 8:97).

5. The Tank Museum has 5 MoD posts out of a staff complement of 61, the Royal Engineers Museum has 5 full-time and 4 part-time out of 12, the Royal Signals Museum has 3 out of 6, while the two Royal Artillery Museums have all of their posts funded by the MoD.

6. Letter from Lieutenant Colonel P.R. Adair to all RHQs, 18 March 1976.

4. The Representation of War

Perhaps one of the points that emerges most strongly from the collection is that most of a soldier's life is spent keeping the peace rather than fighting.
(Caption in the Museum of The King's Regiment, Liverpool)

The one thing that we expect to see in military museums is displays depicting warfare. A military museum without such displays would be unthinkable. It is, after all, as we are led to believe by popular myth, what military life is all about, death or glory on some foreign field of honour. Indeed, army regiments and corps seem particularly determined to emphasize this aspect of their history, with their battle honours on their colours and their barrack blocks named after famous battles in which they took part. Even naval museums have to highlight their depictions of famous engagements at sea, although such battles form a very small part of the naval story.

In fact, of course, warfare has never played more than a relatively minor part statistically in the life of the armed services, and fighting in battles even less so. Indeed it has been claimed that the average regiment will spend five minutes in battle every 50 years[1], while a caption in the National Maritime Museum points out that, in the eighteenth century, 'life (at sea) was routine, much of it was spent in port or blockading enemy ports. A battle was quite a rare occasion', and the nineteenth century was little different. Certainly, before the long-drawn-out carnage of the First World War, it was possible at various periods in our history for a soldier or sailor to serve out his time without hearing a shot fired in anger while serving in a front-line regiment or a ship-of-the-line. With the exception of the Seven Years War, the American Revolution and the French Wars, all of which were fought in a 50-year period, and the Crimean War, which was a brief aberration, the eighteenth and nineteenth centuries were relatively free from major conflicts. There were, of course, a number of colonial wars, but these actually used relatively few British troops and, given the large number of regiments available, a particular unit might go for many years before being called upon to take part in one.

Even during wars, the amount of time spent in battle was very small compared with that spent by the army in marching to and fro about the countryside or laying siege to towns; while the Royal Navy would have spent most of its time blockading ports and sailing the seas looking for the enemy. Even when they met the foe, small-scale skirmishes were a more likely outcome than a full-scale battle. Indeed, Marshal Maurice

61

de Saxe, one of the best-known military theorists of the eighteenth century and himself a highly successful commander, said 'I do not favour pitched battles, and I am convinced that a skilful general could make war all his life without being forced into one' (quoted in Howard 1976:71). Napoleon might not agree, but many military commanders tried to achieve their aims without resorting to the single, unpredictable throw of the dice a battle represented.

In fact sieges, blockades and assaults on fortified positions often played a larger part in military campaigns. Armies could not afford to leave intact strongly held positions threatening their supply lines, while naval blockades were a major way of keeping an enemy fleet tied up in port, or else were an economic weapon used to prevent the enemy from trading by sea. Although such actions did not have the same kudos as battles, the storming of castles, forts, or entrenchments could be equally bloody, and was often as important in winning wars.

The Royal Engineers Museum makes much of these sieges because the Royal Engineers were responsible both for constructing fortified positions and for engineering their downfall. In the museum can be seen models, many of which are some of the earliest parts of the collection, of fortifications and siege works. The Royal Marines Museum has a model and a painting relating to the capture of the Rock of Gibraltar, and its subsequent defence during a four-month siege by Spanish and French forces in 1704. This was the most important success of the Marines up to that point and it remains their one representative battle honour. Many other museums record the part their regiments played in attacking such positions, like, for example, the model in the Royal Green Jackets Museum depicting the storming of the Kasmir Gate of Delhi in 1857, and all of them seem to feature the siege of Sebastopol which lay at the heart of the Crimean War.

Yet, despite the obvious importance in military history of sieges and blockades, it is usually successful battles which are commemorated; railway stations, great houses or barracks are not named after minor skirmishes, blockades or sieges. Battles capture the imagination and the glory, even if, in fact, they are not always the major deciding factor in military campaigns: Agincourt, for example was a glorious victory in an ultimately unsuccessful campaign, and Isandhlwana a terrible defeat in a successful one. But it is in battle that the soldier or sailor makes his most obvious contribution to the security of his country and in which he may win fame and glory or die in the attempt.

But, once it is accepted that battles, and the military campaigns of which they form a part, are considered to be an important element of military history, the problem remains of how to depict them within a museum exhibition. Campaigns can be explained by captions and illustrated using maps, as they are in the Museum of the King's Regiment (Liverpool), or through the interactive fibre optic maps used in the Gurkha Museum. Yet relatively few military museums set these sieges and battles within a clear historical context. The Gurkha Museum does achieve this by using a series of history boards which show what other major events were taking place at the same time as the military conflicts being depicted, while the Regimental Museum of the Queen's Own Hussars begins its displays with a 'time-line' chart which sets the history of the regiment against the major social, political and military events of the period, as does the Royal Norfolk Regimental Museum. The Royal Green Jackets Museum uses captions and maps to set the various battles it describes within the context of the campaign or war of which they were a part, and so does the Lancashire County and Regimental Museum. But few other museums follow suite, and most leave the contextualization to their guide books.

Battles themselves present an almost insurmountable problem for the museum designer and curator. They have two main facets which it is almost impossible to reproduce in a museum display: chaos and violence. The fog of war is an apt phrase when applied to battles. Since cannon were first introduced into warfare in the fourteenth century, there was often a literal fog hanging over parts of the battle, caused by gun smoke. In addition, in many cases, like for example in the battle of Balaclava in 1854, the terrain over which the action took place was so broken and uneven that the commanders could not see what all their forces were doing. Moreover, until recently, communications were so poor and unreliable that, even if the commander could see his troops, there was no guarantee that he could control them. Battles were often, therefore, uncertain affairs where even victory or defeat was not always clear cut.

Battles were large, rambling enterprises, often involving thousands of troops and taking place over many hours or possibly through several days. To encapsulate and to clarify this chaotic action within a museum display is a challenge indeed. Museums usually respond to this by trying to show a snapshot of the battle, or by turning to a representative incident.

The snapshot approach is used by the Royal Green Jackets Museum in Winchester when dealing with the Battle of Waterloo. One gallery is dominated by a magnificent diorama of 20,000 toy soldiers, showing how all the troops on both sides were arranged at a particular moment of the battle (Figure 4.1). A sound and light show then explains how it subsequently developed. A similar model showing that battle, measuring 400 square feet and using 70,000 toy soldiers, and also supplemented by a commentary, is on display in the National Army Museum's 'The Road To Waterloo' gallery. The majority of regimental museums seem to have one or more dioramas showing details of battles in which their regiments were involved.

The Royal Naval Museum has a similar diorama, using small model ships, which shows the Battle of Trafalgar as it stood at 12.45pm on 21 October 1805. This complements a panorama, painted in 1930 by W.L. Wyllie, the leading maritime painter of his day, and his daughter, on what later became the wall of a side gallery to the museum, which shows the battle at 2pm, as though seen from the cabin of the French ship *Neptune* as she retreated.

Figure 4.1 Part of the Waterloo Model in the Royal Green Jackets Museum with
               portraits of distinguished participants in the battle in the background.
Source: Royal Green Jackets Museum

Most military museums use this form of toy soldier diorama, though
some, including the Lancashire County and Regimental Museum, use
cut-out models resembling Victorian children's theatres to achieve the
same effects. Such dioramas have the advantage of allowing a broad
sweep to be depicted in a small area, though they tend to imply an
order to the battle which is unrealistic. They have also been criticized
for their inability to project the magnitude of the battle, and for their
use of one figure to represent a multitude (Jones 1979:82). Moreover,
of course, they cannot convey the movement of the battle, the changes
in fortune, its uncertainty or the human factors of courage and
endurance which are often decisive. This is a miniature world in which
people become pawns, and the whole battle appears like a chess game
being played by God, rather than, as it might have seemed at the time,
a rugby match where much depended on the strength, courage,
determination and skill of the individuals involved.

Similar snapshots of battles or skirmishes are shown in some of the
paintings which line museum walls. Occasionally these paintings try to
show a panorama of the battle. As depictions of the particular battle
they are usually less successful than the dioramas, because they are less
detailed and depict the scene from only one viewpoint. They have the
advantage, though, of being able to show the smoke and the terrain
more successfully than the small models do. Usually, however, artists
prefer to concentrate on a small part of the battle rather than trying to

show the whole. This is particularly true in paintings commissioned by individual regiments, which concentrate on showing a moment in the battle when their regiment carried out a particularly glorious manoeuvre or made a major contribution to the victory.

Military paintings also have the advantage of being much larger than the dioramas, many being of heroic size. This enables them to portray individuals and individual acts of bravery within a particular scene, which gives them a more human face than can be achieved by the dioramas. On the other hand, they are usually works of art as well as depictions of an event, and are full of exaggerations and distortions, as the artist tries to convey the emotion and drama of the event rather than the literal truth. Indeed C. J. ffoulkes (1918:69), the first curator of the Imperial War Museum, remarked in 1918 that 'we have had acres of canvas offered to (the IWM) of battle pictures, the sort of things which make very good illustrations in the illustrated papers, but they are of no value historically. They are painted in a London Studio, and in nine cases out of ten you find a man fallen in a way in which no stricken man ever falls'.

These military paintings were also constrained by the conventions and fashions of their day[2]. Between 1690 and 1790 the representation of warfare was generally highly formalized, with the battle scene little more than a backdrop against which to place a portrait of the most important men present: the King, the general and the senior officers. Towards the end of that period the depiction of the 'soldier-hero' reached its apogee in the numerous death-on-the-battlefield scenes inspired by Benjamin West's painting of the death of General James Wolfe. The dying hero, centre stage, was always shown hand on heart, eyes to heaven, supported by his comrades, while the battle raged in the distance. During this period the artists were very unlikely to have been present at the scene depicted, or even to have visited the battlefield, though they would have drawn on contemporary accounts and sometimes on sketches provided by participants in the battle. The effect sought was heroic rather than truthful, and these paintings, therefore, will tell a visitor to the museum little about the particular battles, though they might give an accurate picture of the uniforms and accoutrements of the period and convey something of the spirit of the age.

The Revolutionary War in America inspired few artists because it would not have been considered tasteful to depict such an unpopular war where Englishman was fighting Englishman. So there is a small gap in many regimental collections for that period, though portraits of officers from that time are still common. But the French Revolutionary and Napoleonic Wars did inspire a large number of paintings and illustrations in newspapers, and so military museums are relatively rich in images of that war. Moreover, these pictures are usually based on accurate representations of the battlefield and of the main participants, as artists visited the scene and sketched the main actors in the drama before attempting their depiction of the event. The battle finally moved to the centre of the stage in these pictures, but the death and destruction was still shown in the subdued way the public had come to expect. Depictions of the death of Nelson and of the Battle of Waterloo proliferated, and were often based on eyewitness accounts, but they marked the end of the grand period of British military paintings.

The public seemed to lose interest in the army for the next 40 years, and military art became a subject for lesser artists. In fact there were few military actions during those years to stir the blood and most regimental museum collections pass quickly over that period. The Crimean War, however, revived interest in military pictures, though, as Peter Harrington (1993:133) observes, 'the tragic events of the war, the bungling of the army hierarchy, and the human suffering particularly among the lower ranks weighed heavily on artistic thinking'; the result was that artists concentrated on the depiction of the common soldier. He was shown dying bravely on the battlefield, but, more unusually, was also depicted in a domestic setting before marching away, and, for practically the first time, his wife might be painted, either taking her leave of him, or hearing the news of his death. Wounded soldiers returning home were also shown, and the theme of the suffering of the serviceman continued to be a popular one in the years immediately after this war.

This style of painting, which predominated for the rest of our period, seems to offer the museum and gallery visitor a more accurate representation of warfare than what was produced for earlier periods. But, even though the emphasis had switched from depicting generals to showing soldiers and battles in close-up, accompanied by a greater stress on the accurate representation of the landscape and of the soldiers' equipment, the image these paintings present of warfare is still not a true one. As a contemporary critic noted, 'The public has no stomach for the gore which runs so freely in French pictures of the sort . . . (and so) . . . the more ghastly aspects of the incidents of war are carefully suppressed' (quoted in Harrington 1993:243). Moreover, to achieve a dramatic effect, the enemy had always to be depicted close at hand, though the nature of contemporary weapons had meant that most battles of the period were actually fought at a distance. All in all the paintings of warfare hanging in regimental museums are usually symbolic and graphic, rather than accurate or truthful snapshots.

Naval museums also have to rely on these snapshot representations of battles. Their use of dioramas has already been mentioned. Paintings also form a significant part of their displays and have attracted a number of major artists. Yet they suffer from the same drawbacks which afflict other military paintings. The panorama pictures of naval battles can be lifeless and make warfare seem much more static than it was in reality, while the individual action paintings often distort the truth by appearing to show the fighting taking place within a small area rather than spread over a few miles as was the reality of such occasions. On the other hand, they often provide striking and powerful images of death and destruction and of noble deeds, and it is hard to see how a naval battle can be better represented in a museum context, except, perhaps, by the use of film.

Recently another form of snapshot has been introduced into military displays: the tableau. These depictions, using dummies and original or, more usually, full-size replicas of equipment, appear in a number of different types of military museum displays, including those relating to battles. In the Royal Scots Regimental Museum in Edinburgh Castle, for example, a sergeant is shown carrying Ensign Kelly from the battle-field, still clutching the regimental colours which he had managed to keep from falling into French hands. The Gurkha Museum has a tableau of a Gurkha soldier in hand-to-hand combat with a Sikh warrior during the First Sikh War in 1846. Clearly these displays can only portray a very small part of the battle, and are usually reserved for the depiction of a single act of bravery by an individual soldier, which is meant to represent all the individual acts of courage which make up a battle. They also give museums an opportunity, by installing audio equipment within the exhibit, to provide some idea of the sounds of battle, as the Regiments of Gloucestershire Museum does with its tableau of Private Crawford saving the colours at the Battle of Salamanca in 1812; of course, the comparatively gentle sounds emanating from such displays convey only an indication of the mind-numbing and ear-splitting cacophony heard on a real battlefield.

An alternative approach, used by the Regimental Museum of the Queen's Own Hussars, is to show the aftermath of the battle. This museum has an excellent tableau showing Captain Walter Unett outside his tent at midday on 14 January 1849, the day after the Battle of Chillianwallah in India during the Sikh Wars, compiling the casualty list of his squadron while still wearing his bloodstained shirt and damaged uniform (Figure 4.2). In this way, the terrible price paid by this unit for the victory is conveyed to the visitor without the need to show the action itself.

Individual tableaux have also been introduced into naval museums. Generally, as in the Royal Naval Museum, they show crew members carrying out their tasks, but they are not used to try to convey an impression of a battle. Arguably these models would be less successful if used as a snapshot of a sea battle than they are for a land one, because most naval battles took place between large fighting ships, with each sailor acting within a specialist team and taking a much less representative part in the fighting than could individual soldiers, though, naturally, individual acts of skill and courage can play an important part in the success of a naval engagement. There are, moreover, possible exceptions to this general rule when, for example, sailors and marines were involved in boarding parties or in landings on foreign shores. On the whole the individual tableau seems less appropriate as a way of depicting a representative incident in naval actions than it is for land battles.

There are, of course, even less satisfactory ways of depicting battles in museum displays. Many military museums merely rely on showing examples of the uniforms worn or the weapons used in particular

Figure 4.2 Tableau in the Regimental Museum of the Queen's Own Hussars:
                Captain Walter Unett outside his tent compiling the casualty list of his
                squadron after the Battle of Chillianwallah.
Source: Regimental Museum of the Queen's Own Hussars

battles, accompanied by a general text describing the action. Yet at least
such case-bound displays can show a variety of original artifacts related
to the battle, which might not be suitable for a tableau and would be
out of place in a diorama. Moreover, a museum full of tableaux and
dioramas depicting similar events might prove just as boring as a
museum dominated by glass cases.

   Arguably cine-film is the best medium in which to show the chaos and
movement of a battle, but that was not available until the Boer War
(Gernsheim 1971:145), and even then technical difficulties, including
the size of the cameras and the need for the cameramen to protect
themselves while operating the hand crank, made it virtually impossible
to film a battle in progress. Indeed, the famous film of the Battle of the
Somme during the First World War had to be made in reserve trenches
using simulated action rather than trying to record the real thing.

Original film is, therefore, not an option for museums to depict battles in the period under review, though remarkable sequences exist from the Second World War and later conflicts which can make very effective audio-visual displays, as the Imperial War Museum has demonstrated. As an alternative there are a few television and motion picture reconstructions of earlier battles available, like the television film of the Battle of Culloden or the cinema film *Zulu* with its reconstruction of the fighting at Rorke's Drift in 1879. But clearly they have to be used with caution and with an adequate explanation for the museum visitor about their limitations as historical sources. The Regimental Museum of the South Wales Borderers has made its own audio-visual display of the part played by its regiment in the Zulu War, and the Border Regiment Museum has several video presentations of campaigns in which the regiment has been involved. Few other museums have so far copied their example.

Given this problem of the presentation of live action, a number of military museums and museums, castles and stately homes with military collections have turned to the staging of reconstructions of battles outside their walls. There now exist in this country a number of societies which stage re-enactments of battles from past wars. The most famous is probably the 'Sealed Knot', originally formed by the late Brigadier Peter Young, a distinguished commando and military historian, which fights battles from the Civil War. All these societies take an inordinate amount of care in their attempts to make the uniforms, weapons, tactics, drill and camp life of the soldiers they portray as accurate as possible.

These re-enactments are, though, no matter how entertaining, merely a form of live tableau. They can provide a very useful teaching aid to show how people of the period looked and the way in which they fought. But the number of participants is far too small to do more than merely represent the opposing armies in any particular battle, and most of the time they will not be fighting over the correct terrain or for the right length of time. As Penny Wilkinson (1993:392) has observed, 'Whilst some societies attain a high standard of display, many battles tend towards pageant and entertainment rather than careful interpretation'. They are, therefore, she concludes, 'scaled down simulations rather than full-scale re-enactments' and because of this 'they have limited value as a method of interpretation for museums'. Moreover, they are also unable to show the harsh and terrible reality of battle. The participants may push and shove each other, collect a few real bruises and sport some stage blood, but they will not actually be blown apart by cannon fire or run through with a sword to die screaming in agony in front of their audience. In other words they fight for their paying customers painless, bloodless and safe small-scale reconstructions of certain battles. They do not show war's reality.

This brings us back to the second problem to be confronted in the representation of warfare: how to portray the effects of its physical violence. It is noticeable that little emphasis is placed in museum displays on the reality of death and injury in battle. Obviously, too much gore may offend members of the public, but not much is even made of the number of casualties in battle. The Guards Museum does display some casualty returns showing the number of guardsmen killed or wounded in certain battles, and the Regiments of Gloucestershire Museum shows a tableau of a wounded soldier being tended by a comrade in its Second World War section, but such direct references to casualties are comparatively rare. Death is usually displayed at one remove. Nelson's bloodstained and holed coat and his blood-soaked breeches and socks are on display in the National Maritime Museum, and similar examples of such artifacts are shown elsewhere. But on the whole a dead soldier or sailor is generally recorded by some memento, like medals or perhaps a personal weapon, while death is described as being 'in action' or 'of wounds' without any specific details.

Death is depicted, of course, in the numerous paintings which adorn the walls of the museums, but, as has already been discussed, it is a stylized and relatively painless death. Photographs can show more of the reality of death, and, of course, much of our knowledge of modern warfare is based on photographic images. But photography was not invented until 1826, and in the middle years of the nineteenth century photographers were using the collodion wet-plate system which required exposures of a minimum of 5–15 seconds to produce a sharp image. It was quite unsuited, therefore, to capturing the movement of battle. By the end of the century the invention of fast-dry plates and the use of smaller, more portable cameras allowed newspaper photographers to capture scenes of battle in the Boer War. But even then there were no official photographers attached to the army, as in later wars, nor amateur photographers serving with units, as became common in the First World War. Therefore, few photographic images of battle enliven the displays in military museums for the period of this study.

Photographs could, though, as has been noted above, show death, for a long exposure time is no disadvantage when photographing corpses. Even then, good taste might prevent photographers from photographing the grotesque and even obscene forms that death can take on the battlefield. In the first systematic photographic coverage of a war, for example, Roger Fenton, a fashionable English photographer with Royal connections, went to the Crimea and produced over 300 photographs. But, although sometimes under fire, he never photographed a battle, nor did he show corpses in his pictures. Most of his images are picturesque scenes or photographs of camp life. Clearly, technical limitations had some influence on his choice of subject, but it has also been claimed (Goldsmith 1979:83) that he avoided unpleasant themes because he wanted to sell his prints to the British public, and because the government, who supported his mission, wanted some good propaganda to counter the unfavourable image created in the public mind by the critical reports from *The Times*' correspondent, William Howard Russell.

Fenton was followed to the Crimea by two amateur photographers, James Robertson, Superintendent and Chief Engineer of the Imperial

Mint in Constantinople, and G. Shaw Lefevre, who both photographed scenes of the destruction resulting from the Siege of Sebastapol. But they also refrained from depicting the human casualties of the war. Robertson later went on to record scenes from the Indian Mutiny in a similar way (Gernsheim 1971:142).

It was the American Civil War, however, which produced the first harrowing images of the death and destruction of a full-scale battle. Mathew Brady, a rich and famous photographer of the day with successful studios in New York and Washington, despatched more than 20 photographers to cover the war, and they sent back horrific images, including bloated corpses with blood oozing from lips and nostrils, which apparently found a ready market with their customers in the North. For better or worse, though, such coverage was not attempted for any of the wars in which Britain was involved until the Boer War, and even then the images sent home were not as gruesome or hard hitting as those produced by Brady.

The portrayal of death is clearly a thorny problem for the military museum. On the one hand current displays either largely ignore it or else show it in a stylized or sanitized form, yet on the other it would seem unnecessarily ghoulish and lacking in taste to fill our military museums with images of human abattoirs. As Sue Wilkinson and Isabel Hughes (1991:25) have asked, 'How do you describe exactly what happened when a bodkin arrow head pierced straight through armour into flesh or illustrate the effects of a Napoleonic cannon on soldiers in the field without becoming horrifically tasteless?' Clearly that is a problem awaiting an imaginative solution.

Of course, not every battle casualty is killed. Many men are wounded and survive. Medical treatment before this century seems barbaric by our standards. Surgery was crude and simple, and without reliable anaesthetics or antiseptics most patients died on the operating table or from infection soon after. But again, little is made of such casualties in museum displays. The National Army Museum has a full-sized model of a discharged wounded soldier reduced to begging after the Napoleonic War, and such images are common in contemporary pictures and books. Moreover, the Royal Army Medical Corps Historical Museum contains some graphic pictures showing the wounds suffered by some of the casualties of the Battle of Waterloo, and has numerous other examples of the effects of bullets and other weapons on the bones of servicemen. But, on the whole, the fate of the wounded either on the battlefield or after is largely ignored in military museums.

More men, moreover, would have died while on campaign from disease and malnutrition than would have been killed in action or died of wounds. Some mention is made, as we shall see in the next chapter, of such casualties, but their fate does not play a large part in the depiction in museums of military campaigns or naval expeditions.

The other main category of battle casualty, the prisoner of war (POW), has a slightly higher profile in military museums, but it is generally enemy POWs who are mentioned. The Royal Naval Museum, for example, has models of prison hulks in which French POWs were kept during the Napoleonic Wars. More interestingly, it also has a number of examples of the carved models of ships, ships in bottles and decorated horns, known collectively as scrimshaw work, produced by these French POWs during their captivity as a way of whiling away the time and of supplementing their income. In the Regiments of Gloucestershire Museum a modern equivalent of this type of POW work is shown for a British soldier, as on display is a stone cross and a badge carved by Colonel James Carne VC to occupy his time while a POW in Korea. But on the whole in the period up to 1914 little mention is made of British POWs, though a photograph of Private John Dryden, a British POW from the Charge of the Light Brigade, is featured in the Royal Hussars Museum. If regimental museums are largely family affairs, as Stephen Woods claims, then it is to be expected that these more negative aspects of the experience of war should not receive much coverage in their displays.

Military defeats and blunders are not likely to appear either, unless as a way of highlighting the courage of the men involved. The Museum of the Duke of Edinburgh's Royal Regiment, for example, has a display commemorating the men of the 66th Foot, who were killed during the British defeat in the Battle of Maiwand in Afghanistan on 27 July 1880, as they had held firm while other troops in the force had turned and ran, leaving them facing impossible odds. The Royal Naval Museum, moreover, has a small display of ship models relating to the successes of John Paul Jones, the American Revolutionary War naval captain, in his sea battles against the British, and there is another series of cases recording American naval victories in the single ship actions of the War of 1812. The National Maritime Museum, however, has a short video film which discusses Dutch victories against the Royal Navy in the seventeenth century. The National Army Museum has a model depicting the British defeat at Yorktown during the American Revolutionary War and paintings depicting the defeat at Isandhlwana during the Zulu War. But on the whole, as might be expected, even the national museums say little about defeats. Their displays also do not tackle subjects like cowardice or desertion.

By the same token they say little about the effect of these pre-twentieth-century wars on the civilian population of Britain, or the dependence of the military effort on the civilian economy, subjects which will be dealt with in more detail later in this book. It is not to be expected that these topics would be touched on in the regimental museums. These regiments were formed after the English Civil War and, apart from the campaigns in Ireland in 1689–90 and the two brief Jacobite uprisings, there was little fighting directly affecting this land from then until the aerial attacks of the First World War. The regiments had, therefore, little contact with British civilians in wartime in this earlier period and so are unlikely to mention them in their displays.

It is also noticeable, though, that military museums in this country, while containing a lot of personal mementos of famous men, do not, in fact, tell us much about their contribution to the waging of war. As has been said above, warfare is often a confused business, and battles may be decided by luck, by changes in the weather, by errors made by the enemy, or by the courage of individual soldiers and sailors. Yet it is naive to suggest that the skill and knowledge of military commanders always play an insignificant part in this process, and it is disappointing that their strategic and tactical skills are not discussed and explained in more detail in military museum displays.

It is true that the naval museums do touch on this topic and tell their visitors, for example, something of the tactics used by Nelson to defeat the French and Spanish fleets in his famous engagements. In France the displays on Napoleon in the Hôtel des Invalides talk about the way he won his battles, but in this country the National Army Museum tells us virtually nothing in its exhibitions about the tactical skills of Marlborough or Wellington or our other leading generals.

Such information may be found within the stately homes of British military figures like Apsley House and Blenheim Palace. And perhaps it could be argued that these personal shrines are a more appropriate place to celebrate the genius of these individuals. Yet museum displays seem to give a very narrow view of these battles when no explanation or analysis is provided of the strategy or tactics used in fighting them.

This is probably a result of two complementary effects. The first is the undoubted lack of display space in most military museums. An analysis of each major battle would impose a tremendous strain on the available exhibition area and could turn the walls of military museums into unimaginably dull textbooks. It is unlikely, moreover, that the majority of people would want to read in considerable detail about the way in which each battle was planned and fought. But to give greater depth to these displays, and to prevent them being merely a glorification of courage or the commemoration of the dead, an attempt should be made, I feel, to examine the way in which some of the major battles in our history were planned and executed.

The other factor operating against such displays is the movement away from the 'Great Man' approach to history over the last 30 years. It is no longer acceptable to try to explain every achievement in history as the work of certain famous individuals. This applies equally to military history, and may help to explain why museums refrain from describing the wars of the early eighteenth century in terms of the achievements of Marlborough, and depicting the Napoleonic War in terms of the successes of Wellington.

Quite rightly, more emphasis is now placed on the lives and actions of ordinary men and women, and it is their trials and their achievements which have become the centrepiece of museum displays. This fits very well, of course, with the ethos of regimental museums, which are bound to be more concerned with the history of their soldiers than they are with some more distant commander. The way in which the individual lives of soldiers and sailors in peace and war are depicted in military museums is the subject of the next chapter.

Notes

1. Peter Russell-Jones, curatorial advisor to Hampshire's military museums (quoted in Greene, 1991:13).
2. Much of the following is based on Harrington (1993).

5. *The Life of the Serviceman*

History and experience prove all too clearly that the common fighting man is apt to be soon forgotten.

(Museums Journal 1917 16,10:244)

The main thrust of military history has always been the study of warfare. Tactics and strategy have been examined in some detail and lessons have been drawn from them. Moreover, in recent years a plethora of books have been produced examining the weaponry and hardware used in battle. Military museums have tended to follow this trend, with displays depicting particular campaigns and individual battles, with supporting cases concentrating on weapons, uniforms, transport and the other machines of war.

The individual serviceman has been largely left out. It is true, of course, that his commanders have been given considerable space in these displays[1]. Even though, as was discussed in the previous chapter, little has been done effectively to show how they fought and won their battles or planned their campaigns, a considerable quantity of iconographic material has been brought together to celebrate their lives. The uniforms, telescopes, personal weapons, camp furniture and other memorabilia, together with the more exotic possessions of famous generals and admirals, are spread fairly evenly around our regimental and national museums.

Perhaps the finest collection of such mementos is that shared between the Royal Naval Museum and the National Maritime Museum, which consists of objects that had belonged to Admiral Lord Nelson. This great man died a hero's death and his friends and family were anxious to preserve anything which reminded them of him. His uniforms, accoutrements, furniture and other personal items therefore survive and are on display. One can see the cutlery that had to be specially made for him because of the loss of his arm and a number of the other personal items he would have used at sea. Yet there is little attempt in either museum to draw any general lessons about life at sea from these objects. They are merely curios, part of the hagiography of this great man.

The ordinary soldier or sailor is most commonly represented in regimental and service museums in their Medal Galleries. Gallantry awards, long service and campaign medals are displayed. Some museums, like that of the Royal Marines, put together groups which include a common gallantry or campaign medal and give a brief explanation of the origin of that award. Others, including the Royal Signals Museum, like to arrange the medals according to family or unit connections. Most museums provide some brief biographical information about the recipients of the medals, but it generally only includes details about their birth, death and the units with which they served, although it can be quite extensive in the case of Victoria Cross (VC) winners. The importance of these Medal Galleries for the units, and for the families of those whose medals are displayed there, cannot be overstated. These displays symbolize the service and sacrifice of these servicemen and women and act as their permanent memorial. But this is a 'family' display which may mean little to ordinary visitors, who are unlikely to learn much about the life of these servicemen in such a gallery.

Indeed, what is lacking in most military museum displays is the sense of the real men behind the uniforms. These sailors and soldiers spent most of their adult lives in the armed forces, and, as has already been stated, only a relatively small part of this time was likely to be spent on campaign, and even less in action. In the comparatively longer periods when they were not fighting or dying they had lives to lead, and it is this day-to-day existence which needs to be explored in museum displays more fully if a closer connection is to be made between the experiences of the museum visitors and those of their ancestors in uniform.

The picture is not totally bleak. Museum displays have begun to tackle this topic in the last decade, though it is still more common to find depictions of the daily lives of officers than of their men, partly because of the uneven nature of the survival of artifacts, which was discussed in Chapter 1. But it is possible, perhaps, by visiting a number of military museums, to build up a reasonable picture of the military life of both officers and men in this period.

Life for the serviceman starts before he ever joins the forces. The Gurkha Museum in Winchester begins its exhibition with displays which set the Gurkha soldier within his Nepalese social and cultural background. It looks at the agricultural setting from which these troops have traditionally been drawn and shows how the hardship of this kind of existence prepares the soldier for his life in the army. Most other military museums do not tackle this topic, though the Regiments of Gloucestershire Museum gives a breakdown of the occupations of those who entered that regiment at different times, and thereby provides a good indication of the types of backgrounds from which these soldiers came. The displays in the Military Museum of Devon and Dorset also include a series of tableaux which compare the clothing, equipment and incomes of soldiers from three different years, 1855, 1914 and 1994, with those of the farm workers of the same periods, thereby setting them in their socio-historical context. Sailors can normally be assumed to have come from a nautical background, though a caption in the Royal Naval Museum explains that 50 per cent would have been pressed into service and another 12 per cent would have been supplied by the local parishes to a fixed government quota, probably from the gaols. Moreover, in the case of the officers, this assumption may not always have been correct, as the example of Nelson, the son of a village rector from Norfolk, demonstrates.

Next, the agricultural labourer, blacksmith or poor clerk had to be recruited into the armed forces. As the Regiments of Gloucestershire Museum explains in one of its captions, hunger and unemployment were often the main stimuli to enlistment for the ordinary serviceman, though others may have been escaping from criminal proceedings (or, like the quota sailor, being given the choice between a term in the armed forces or in prison), from family responsibilities or from debt. As a result, until the latter part of the nineteenth century, the armed forces were mainly recruited from the very poorest, most ignorant or most criminal sections of society (Barnett 1970:313). The most notorious recruiting agents in the eighteenth and early nineteenth centuries were the recruiting parties and the press gangs. Both used underhand methods, such as getting prospective recruits drunk or resorting to trickery and violence, to acquire the men they needed to fill their quotas (Hackett 1962:27). Such antics are shown in contemporary paintings and prints, some of which hang in military museums, but rarely is this feature of service history emphasized in displays.

Officers were not recruited in this way, of course, and had, in fact, to buy their commissions in cavalry and infantry units before 1871 (except in the specialist corps or the Royal Navy). They were unlikely to be paupers, therefore, but were sometimes family or social outcasts, children, adventurers, or idiots who could obtain no other employment (Turner 1956:21). While their actions and achievements are described in military museums, their characters, backgrounds and reasons for joining the armed forces are usually not.

Having been recruited, by whatever means, the men had to be trained to fulfil their role. This is another topic which receives surprisingly little attention in most military museums. General training is dealt with by the Aldershot Military Museum, as Aldershot was the main training camp for the British Army for many years. But, on the whole, this initial period of service, and the frequent reinforcing training exercises soldiers would have endured throughout their service life, are not shown. Basic training, with its emphasis on order, discipline and weapons skills, is an important period in a soldier's or sailor's life, as are the numerous mock battles and other exercises that they have to undergo. But training and manoeuvres tend to feature only in a few of the paintings and prints which adorn the museums' walls. The Royal Green Jackets Museum uses illustrated captions to discuss training and the development of infantry tactics, but is unusual in this respect.

In fact, despite the large number of weapons which fill display cases in military museums, there is often little mention of the way in which the serviceman was trained to use this most basic of all his tools, nor any discussion of the way these tools performed. The agricultural museum will usually explain the workings of the plough or the seed-drill, and the town museum may give some information about the myriad of kitchen implements, but the rifle, pistol, sword and bayonet seem to be taken for granted in most regimental museums, probably because the 'family' members and military buffs who traditionally make up the majority of visitors to these museums will already be familiar with at least some of these weapons.

This is not always the case, of course, and some museums ensure that these tools are explained. As we shall see in Chapter 9, the Royal Naval Museum and the National Maritime Museum explain the construction, development and use of the sailor's main tool, the ship, in considerable detail. They also look at naval weapons and describe how they were used. Some army museums also see the need to discuss or describe these weapons. The Guards Museum, for example, has a fine life-sized tableau of a pikeman and a musketeer of the late seventeenth century supported by an enlargement of an illustrated drill showing how both weapons were to be used. A similar drill shown on a silk handkerchief for the 1893 Lee Metford rifle is displayed in the National Army Museum.

Other museums try to give their visitors an idea of the efficiency of these tools. The Museum of the Regiments of Gloucestershire shows the rate of fire of the standard British infantry musket of the Napoleonic era and discusses its accuracy. A more graphic illustration of the same theme is contained in the National Army Museum's 'The Road to Waterloo' exhibition, where a life-sized model shows Private Matthew Clay, 3rd Foot Guards, at the Battle of Waterloo loading his musket by biting off the end of the paper cartridge, which contained the gunpowder and musket ball, prior to pouring it into the barrel. The accompanying caption notes that, in his account of the battle, Clay remarks that his musket frequently misfired, because its wooden stock had swollen in the rain and kept jamming the lock. He also recorded that he was shot at several times from close range by French skirmishers, but was never hit, which gives a pretty good indication of the true accuracy of these weapons. An even more exciting way of conveying information about these weapons is used by the Royal Green Jackets Museum, which has an electronic firing range where 'the visitor can handle an exact replica of a Baker rifle and engage advancing light infantry in a realistic landscape setting'[2]. This museum also has displays showing how the rifle developed during this period (figure 5.1). However, probably the best exhibition of personal weapons in this country, which is in the Weapons Museum in the School of Infantry at Warminster, is only open to the public by appointment.

Perhaps not surprisingly, I have not come across a museum which offers visitors the chance to use a replica sword or bayonet, though occasionally children are allowed to feel the weight of such weapons in handling sessions, and illustrated fencing drills are displayed in some museums. The Regimental Museum of the 9th/12th Royal Lancers also has an interesting caption which explains the development and use of the cavalry lance. Moreover, the Museum of Artillery shows the way in which guns evolved throughout this period, and the Royal Armouries have fine collections of swords and other weapons. But on

Figure 5.1 Rifle display in the Royal Green Jackets Museum showing the development of this weapon from 1838 to 1940.

Source: Royal Green Jackets Museum

the whole it seems to be assumed that visitors to military museums will already know all they want to about the way in which these tools of the serviceman's trade were used and developed.

Having gone through their basic training and learned to use their weapons, the soldier or sailor could be called upon, after further specialist training, to perform a number of tasks, particularly after the Napoleonic Wars, when the increased importance of technology in a rapidly industrializing world was reflected in the armed forces by an increase in the number of technical branches. As the variety of corps museums demonstrate, for example, soldiers could now be employed as armourers, cooks, medical orderlies, drivers, signallers, clerks and accountants, as well as infantrymen, gunners and engineers. Sailors could be carpenters, shipwrights, cooks, navigators, signallers or gunners and undertake a variety of other specialized tasks, all of which need to be shown and explained in the naval museums. These specialists will be discussed in more detail in Chapter 6.

Obviously, being human, there were times when these men made mistakes or committed crimes. Society was harsh in the 250 years covered by this survey, and the armed forces reflected this. Punishment was severe. Both the Royal Marines Museum and the Guards Museum display a cat-o'-nine-tails which was used to give up to 2000 lashes to servicemen found guilty of a variety of offences, from theft to insubordination, between 1689 and 1880 (Barnett 1970:241,309). The procedure adopted for administering this punishment is described in the Regiments of Gloucestershire Museum and in other museums, though, perhaps not surprisingly, this is usually done by the use of captions, not models. The Military Museum of Devon and Dorset, though, has made good use of one of the rooms of the Keep in which it is situated, to set up a tableau of a soldier, lying on his front on a bunk in his cell, showing the marks of the lash across his back. In the Guards Museum can also be seen a spring-loaded device for branding a deserter, and the Royal Army Medical Corps Historical Museum has on display a piece of skin taken from a corpse during an autopsy, which shows how effective this branding was. The Guards Museum also mentions that the death penalty would be used for more serious offences. The Regimental Museum of the 9th/12th Royal Lancers, on the other hand, makes the important point in one of its captions that some petty crimes, like theft from a comrade or repeated drunkenness, were often dealt with by the men themselves with 'barrack room courts martial' which would hand out quite severe penalties.

Occasionally soldiers or sailors reacted to harsh conditions and mutinied, demanding better pay or food or less harsh punishments. This is dealt with by the Royal Marines Museum in relation to the Spithead and Nore naval mutinies of 1797, but is not a topic usually touched on by military museums, though the Royal Scots Regimental Museum admits that it was a revolt within that regiment which led to the introduction of the separate body of Military Law.

Some of the grievances leading to such mutinies related to accommodation. Sailors lived and worked in appallingly restricted conditions until this century. This is remarked on but not really demonstrated in the main naval museums, though a good idea of these cramped quarters can be gained by visiting HMS *Victory*, or HMS *Warrior* in Portsmouth Dockyard (Figure 5.2), or, in a less satisfactory way, by looking at the display on the naval mutinies in the Royal Marines Museum, which depicts a section of a gun deck where the sailors spent all their time.

Soldiers lived in inns or requisitioned barns and stables until the 1790s. To illustrate this phase of the soldier's history, a tableau in the Scottish United Services Museum shows Major John Dalgleish of the 21st Regiment of Foot in his cramped quarters in the Abercorn Inn, Paisley, in January 1797, surrounded by his personal possessions and military equipment. At that time fear of invasion by the French led to the building of barracks so that troops could be concentrated together at strategic places. Later barracks were built near the major cities to enable troops to be on hand to put down civil disturbances, as the Museum of the Manchesters explains when discussing the reasons for the building of the barracks in Ashton-under-Lyne in 1843.

Figure 5.2 Crew's quarters on the Gun Deck of HMS *Warrior* showing hammocks slung above the guns and the dining tables.
Source: Peter Thwaites

Before the middle of the nineteenth century these barracks were usually cold, cramped buildings. As the Regiments of Gloucestershire Museum explains, overseas barracks were generally larger to allow for the circulation of air, but barracks in this country were small and crowded, with the result that disease could rapidly spread from one occupant to another. As the historian Corelli Barnett (1970:280), has pointed out, while in the 1840s a convict in a cell in a British gaol would enjoy 1000 cubic feet of air, a soldier in a home barracks would have only 3–400 cubic feet. As a result his life expectancy was lower than his civilian counterpart's, with the death rate from tuberculosis, for instance, being five times higher amongst soldiers than in the rest of the population.

A barrack display from 1900 is shown in the Aldershot Military Museum (Figure 5.3) and a reconstruction of a barrack room in India is amongst the exhibits of the Lancashire County and Regimental Museum. But, while these exhibits give some idea of the way in which these barracks were arranged, they are a little too sanitized to give an accurate picture of life in one of these buildings. It is perhaps asking too much, though, to expect a museum to be able to convey the true conditions in a living space through a static display.

These barracks were, of course, the living areas of the ordinary soldiers. The officers, although not well off by our standards, lived much easier lives. Even on naval ships the officers had more space in which to sleep, live and eat than their men, and were housed in more salubrious parts of the ship, as the surviving examples of Royal Navy warships show. They also usually slept in bunks rather than hammocks and might have

Figure 5.3 Barrack Room scene, *c.* 1900, in the Aldershot Military Museum.
Source: Aldershot Military Museum

had lockers in which to keep a few personal belongings. The army officer, when not on campaign, would be surrounded in his mess by good furniture and paintings, and would eat off good quality china on a table decorated with silver candlesticks and centrepieces. Officers' mess displays are popular in regimental museums, as they allow the display of some of the museum's collection of mess dress from different periods, mess furniture and mess silver. The King's Own Scottish Borderers Regimental Museum shows a mock-up of a complete Mess Dining Room from about 1900 in all its splendour, and several museums have similar tableaux. In a few cases, such as the Royal Marines Museum, the museum is actually situated *in* an old officers' mess, which gives a good idea of the grandeur of some of these buildings in comparison to the barn-like soldiers' accommodation. The Regimental Museum of the Queen's Own Hussars shows an officer's room in the Cavalry Barracks at Aldershot in 1871 with the incumbent dressing for dinner and talking to his guest from a sister regiment. It gives that museum a good opportunity to display bedroom furniture and fittings from the period and to convey something of the way in which officers lived while serving in Britain.

There is little information in any of these museums about the way in which officers and men would have lived while on active service. Captain Walter Unett is shown outside his tent in the tableau in the Regimental Museum of the Queen's Own Hussars, and the Duke of Wellington's Regimental Museum has a reconstruction of a Crimean War hut, while most museums have examples of camp beds, cooking utensils and other camp furniture. But displays showing living conditions when on campaign are rare.

In the same way, although the Lancashire County and Regimental Museum has an Indian barrack-room tableau illustrating life in that outpost of empire, few others mount similar displays, and most rely on displaying appropriate uniforms and curios to convey the soldier's life on overseas postings. Yet at any one time over half of the British Army would have been serving abroad, and India, in particular, was an important base. As Corelli Barnett (1970:278) has said, 'by 1850 India had become the greatest formative influence on the life, language and legend of the British Army, for most British soldiers could expect to serve there, and for a long time'. They led a very different life there compared with a home posting. There were servants, better accommo-dation and greater leisure opportunities to set against the hardship caused by the alien conditions, the constant threat of disease and the other dangers of a foreign posting. The Royal Hussars Museum uses a mock-up of an Indian verandah to introduce a large display of photo-graphs taken during the regiment's long service in India, which helps to convey something of the life led in that second home of the British Army, as do the photographs, paintings, uniforms and other artifacts on display at the British in India Museum in Colne.

The accommodation for officers and men discussed above was designed primarily for the single man. The Regiments of Gloucestershire Museum, as we shall see in the next chapter, shows a representation of a married soldier's end of the barracks. One must assume that the family life of the soldier, whose wife and family were not on the strength, like the sailor's and the officer's, was lived at the level in society appro-priate to the background from which he came. This is not discussed in military museums for this period, though some military paintings of the late nineteenth century show domestic scenes, and both the Museum of the Royal Highland Fusiliers and the Royal Engineers Museum have reconstructions of rooms in twentieth-century soldiers' homes.

It is perhaps not surprising that sexual relations are not touched upon in these museum displays. They do not feature, for example, in similar social history museums to any great extent, though it is a topic which is currently receiving more attention (see *Museums Journal* 1994 94,2:29). But the Regiments of Gloucestershire Museum display begs the question of how a married couple could enjoy their marital relations when only separated from the rest of the barrack room by a blanket. Moreover, soldiers and sailors were notoriously licentious. Victorian folk songs are full of young ladies being seduced in sentry boxes or abandoned by their sailor lovers, while soldiers and sailors frequently visit prostitutes. An even darker side of their reputation is shown in the stories of rapes carried out by soldiers or sailors, particularly when abroad (Barnett 1970:242). Yet none of this appears to be discussed, even in the national museums. Perhaps most military museum trustees believe that this is a topic best left to the military historian working in the archives, rather than being exposed to the gaze of the schoolchild in the galleries.

On the other hand, the army's own answer to excess energy – sport – features prominently in regimental museums. Faced with a number of active young men who had a tendency to turn to drink or sexual indulgence when not fully occupied, the military authorities first tried hard, monotonous work to keep them occupied, backed up with harsh punishment if this failed. But by the nineteenth century they realized that organized sport was a much better way to absorb this energy. Sport was, after all, also a good way of keeping the men fit. It encouraged the development of team spirit, which is a vital military attribute, and competition, which kept the men on their toes.

Most sport was regimentally based, and so military museum displays usually contain a broad range of sporting equipment and sporting trophies. The Museum of the Duke of Edinburgh's Royal Regiment has a fine case of such trophies, and they are featured in the displays of most regimental, corps and service museums.

Until the late nineteenth century there was a social division within sport. Officers and men did not compete, as that would have been considered bad for morale, and in any case they tended to take part in different sports. Officers hunted, rode, fenced, played polo and tennis, while the men ran, played football and boxed. The trophies reflect these differences, but the museum captions often do not comment upon them. They do highlight, however, the valuable contribution such sports were thought to make to developing and maintaining regimental pride and cohesion.

Sport was, of course, not always the most appropriate way to fill in time. For the sailor on board ship, or for the older man, or in inclement weather, other pastimes must have seemed more attractive, as they do today. The Royal Naval Museum and the National Maritime Museum contain interesting examples of the handicrafts practised by sailors in their spare time, while the National Army Museum displays similar examples of soldiers' handicrafts which, it explains, were encouraged by the military authorities to prevent the soldiers from turning to drink. Macramé, embroidery, carvings in wood and bone, examples of poetry, drawings, paintings and useful handmade items like brushes, combs, and pots and pans abound in displays in these and other military museums. They show, together with musical instruments like the concertina carried by Surgeon James Fairweather during the Indian Mutiny displayed in the National Army Museum, that the servicemen, at least occasionally, had more on their minds than just drink and sex when they were not involved in their military duties!

Some of these objects made in the soldier's or sailor's spare time would have been intended for sale to augment the meagre income he gained from his main occupation. Both the Regiments of Gloucestershire Museum and the National Army Museum give the rates of pay for soldiers at different times during the period under review, while the Royal Naval Museum does the same for sailors. The Regiments of Gloucestershire Museum usefully compares these with those earned by a labourer at the same time. The comparisons cannot hope to be exact, because the soldier sometimes received a uniform and some other benefits that the labourer would have had to provide for himself. But on the whole these captions show how poorly paid the serviceman was, particularly as stoppages for food, barrack repairs, the replacement cost of equipment and many other items that he needed could easily wipe out most of what he theoretically received each week. Corelli Barnett (1970:241,280) has estimated that, while the soldier nominally earned one shilling a day in the early nineteenth century, deductions would have left him with 2¾d a day to save or spend, while a bricklayer in the same period would have been earning over three shillings gross. These stoppages could be even worse for the cavalry soldier, as the Regimental Museum of the 9th/12th Royal Lancers explains, because he would also have had to pay for forage for his horse, meet veterinary bills and make a contribution towards the purchase of unit remounts.

A National Army Museum caption makes it clear that officers were also generally paid very little for their services. A colonel would receive £1 per day and an ensign five shillings, which might sound a reasonable sum, but out of that they would have to find the cost of their uniform and pay their mess bills and other expenses. Moreover the colonel may well have paid £20,000 for his command and the ensign £500 for his commission. Both also had to pay a high premium for any subsequent promotions, unless they were gained for merit in the field. The National Army Museum points out that in the Regency and early Victorian period, in particular, changes in uniform were frequent and, as a result, officers needed to be independently wealthy to bear this expense, particularly in one of the more fashionable and flamboyant guards or cavalry regiments.

It is small wonder, therefore, that soldiers and their officers indulged in looting while on campaign, or that sailors, who were equally poorly paid, should have been so anxious to capture enemy vessels for which they would be given prize money (Turner 1956:101–9).

The amount of money available to the serviceman would affect his diet. While an officer would be eating good food from fine china in the wardroom or mess, the ordinary serviceman would partake of much simpler fare. The Royal Marines Museum shows examples of the ship's biscuit and meat ration eaten by the Marines from their square pieces of bread and, later, square dishes (from which comes the expression 'three square meals a day'). It seems pretty poor fare by our standards, and would not have been made more appetizing by the presence of weevils and other insects that, the Museum shows, often infested it. The Royal Naval Museum describes the sailor's weekly food ration, which seems adequate by the standards of the day, though, of course, its quality and the way it would have been prepared cannot be demonstrated and must be left to the visitor's imagination. Before the move into barracks, soldiers were generally fed on gristly meat and potatoes supplied by their unwilling hosts. Later, in barracks, they were normally given two meals a day, breakfast and a dinner in the middle of the day, the total daily ration being one pound of bread and three quarters of a pound of meat. They then filled their stomachs in the evening with beer or grog. Just before the Crimean War, a third meal was introduced, for which the soldiers had to pay, as they did for any food provided in addition to the bread and meat.

Before the creation of the Army Catering Corps, soldiers frequently had to cook their own meals when on campaign, or, in the case of officers, have them cooked by their batmen. The Guards Museum displays the canteen pannier, containing a selection of pewter plates and dishes used by Captain the Hon. Orlando Bridgeman, 1st Foot Guards, in Spain and at the Battle of Waterloo, and a spirit stove used by Lieutenant Colonel the Lord Herbert Scott during the Boer War. The Regimental Museum of the 9th/12th Royal Lancers has a display for the Boer War which shows the field rations for a soldier of one and a half pounds of bread, one pound of fresh, salt or preserved meat and the other parts of the allowance. While on campaign soldiers had to rely on an inefficient commissariat which often failed, as numerous museums explain, to provide even these minimum rations; looting might be the only way starvation could be prevented.

The serviceman's health was clearly a matter partly under the control of his masters. This was, however, a time when preventive medicine was in its infancy. British soldiers were more likely to die from disease than their civilian contemporaries, because of their poor food and the insanitary conditions in which they lived. This was compounded by the frequent moves that a soldier or sailor would have to make, all over the British empire. Sea voyages, far from the healthy pastimes now advertised in travel brochures, were, for the servicemen forced to endure them, long and dangerous experiences. The ship in which they travelled might founder, as many did in this period. Such a tragedy is recorded in the Military Museum of Devon and Dorset with a display concerning the troop-ship *Sarah Sands*, which in November 1857 caught fire 800 miles off the Indian coast while carrying soldiers of the 54th Foot and their families. And the Royal Green Jackets Museum has a display case called 'In peril on the sea' in which it gives examples of six disasters and near disasters suffered by the regiment since 1849. But it was even more likely that servicemen or their families would succumb to cholera or one of the other deadly diseases which could ravage crowded troopships or ships-of-the-line. Corelli Barnett (1970:144) has claimed, in fact, that in the eighteenth century the wastage of men and horses in sea transit was so appalling that large-scale British movement was as advantageous to the French as a British defeat in battle!

Once arrived at his destination, the soldier might find himself in a country which looked like a tropical paradise, but which contained a whole host of exotic diseases for which he had no immunity and his leaders no cures, even though the Royal Army Medical Corps Historical Museum demonstrates in its displays that many army surgeons died trying to find such cures. The National Army Museum, through the use of a model of a stricken soldier of the 13th (1st Somersetshire) Regiment of Foot suffering from yellow fever in the Caribbean in 1795, highlights this danger, and the accompanying caption explains that soldiers were much more likely to die of sickness than be killed in battle. As an example, it records the high death rate from disease in the West Indies, over 60,000 in two years in the 1790s; this led the authorities to lie to their men as to their ultimate destination when sending them there, to prevent them from mutinying. But this was only one of many danger spots. As the National Army Museum introduction to 'The Road To Waterloo' exhibition explains, troops might be moved frequently between a number of different locations, thus giving them little chance to become properly acclimatized, and thereby increasing their chances of falling prey to a host of foreign diseases or to the effects of alien climatic conditions.

The equipment with which they were issued was also not up to the task of protecting them against the conditions in which they were forced to serve. Throughout the late Stuart period the colonel of the regiment was responsible for clothing his regiment, and was given an allowance from which to do so. An unscrupulous colonel could make a fat profit by providing his men with the bare minimum of poor quality clothing and pocketing the difference (Barnett 1970:143). After 1708 some control was imposed on the quality and quantity of the uniforms supplied, and they gradually improved. As has been stated, however, uniforms changed frequently in the eighteenth and nineteenth centuries, and were designed more for appearance than for function. King George II had begun this trend by insisting that soldiers' uniforms looked dashing and attractive, even though the changes he introduced made them much less serviceable than before. Again the excellent series of National Army Museum models shows soldiers sweating in uniforms which were too thick for the tropics and freezing in uniforms which were too flimsy for the cold of Canada. Surprisingly enough, given the frequent criticism of military museums for giving too much space to the study of obscure bits of uniform, few actually explain what the different pieces of uniform and kit were for, nor do they discuss their development over time. Changes in uniform are shown by using model soldiers in both the Museum of the Duke of Edinburgh's Royal Regiment and the Royal Marines Museum, while the National Army Museum is able to demonstrate these developments by using actual examples from all periods. But military museums do not usually discuss the strengths and weaknesses of different designs, and seem content instead to show glorious examples of ceremonial uniforms and accoutrements. Yet, as the Regiments of Gloucestershire Museum makes plain, it was the public outcry caused by the inadequacies of the uniforms issued to Crimean War soldiers, as much as their poor food, and bad housing and health care, which led to the inquiries and eventual reforms which changed the lives of late nineteenth-century soldiers for the better[3].

Overall, therefore, little actually appears in most military museum displays about the health of these servicemen. The Royal Marines Museum exhibits a discharge book of 1786 to 1791 which lists the reasons why men were dismissed from the service, and draws attention to the number who were considered medically unfit to continue. Other museums discuss health in general terms, but it is left, as will be shown in the next chapter, to the specialist museums to demonstrate how attempts were made to cure sickness or to keep the serviceman healthy in this period.

As the Royal Marines Museum discharge book shows, however, a time would inevitably come when the soldier had either completed the number of years for which he had signed on, or had become unfit for duty, though a large number would, of course, have been killed in action or died of disease before reaching that time. Few military museums, however, tell their visitors about the fate of ex-soldiers, except anecdotally and accidentally when describing the life of a VC winner or some other notable character. The National Army Museum, on the other hand, provides a model of a soldier of the 27th Inniskilling Regiment in 1825, wounded in the Battle of Waterloo, who was unable to work at his trade on his discharge from the army, and was forced to beg in the streets of London to supplement his very meagre pension. At the same time its audio-visual exhibit tells the story of three Victorian soldiers. One of them was killed in action, but the other two found employment after their service was over. Of these, though, one was frequently in financial difficulties and had to ask for supplements to his pension. A caption in the Royal Green Jackets Museum also highlights the hardships these ex-soldiers had to endure on their meagre pensions. But perhaps the most poignant symbol of this is a pawn ticket for 10 shillings, dated September 1886, held in the Royal Hampshire Regiment Museum, which was given to Lieutenant E.H. Lenon, late of the 67th Regiment of Foot, when he was forced to pawn a silver medal and the Victoria Cross he had won at the Taku Forts in China in 1860. Clearly the ex-serviceman's lot was unlikely to be a happy one in many cases.

On the other hand, a few hundred soldiers who had become unfit for duty, either after 20 years' service or as a result of wounds, might be lucky enough to end their days as in-Pensioners in the Royal Hospital, Chelsea, founded by King Charles II in 1682. Its museum, which was set up in 1960, contains medals and uniforms of those Pensioners who have lived in the Royal Hospital over the last 300 years. A similar institution for sailors, the Royal Naval Hospital at Greenwich, was founded in 1694, but closed in 1869. Its building was taken over by the Royal Naval College in 1873 but some of the main rooms were left unaltered and are now open to the public.

In the end, how full a picture do military museums paint of the daily life of servicemen in the period of this review? As we have seen, they are strong on some parts of the experience and weaker on others. Anyone interested in the topic, who could not gain access to relevant books, would be able, by visiting a number of military museums, to discover why men joined the army or navy, how they were trained, where they served and how they finished their service. One could also find out something about their food, accommodation, clothing, pay and pensions. Specialist museums, as will become clear in the next chapter, would tell the visitor about the serviceman's medical care, specialized training, education and other aspects of his life and that of the camp followers who would accompany him wherever he went.

This seems on the face of it to be an extensive and fairly complete picture. There are, of course, some areas not touched on in much detail, perhaps either through delicacy or from a desire not to misrepresent by giving a sensational but atypical picture. On the whole, it could be argued that at least as full a picture of the life and work of the serviceman can be gleaned from these museums as may appear about the life of the farm labourer in most rural life museums, or the average factory worker (if such a creature exists) in the numerous industrial heritage sites which now cover our landscape.

It is not easy, of course, in any case, to successfully convey the realities of someone's life through a static display, though photographs can perhaps give a flavour of daily life from the Victorian period onwards. Indeed the Royal Norfolk Regimental Museum uses a combination of captions and photographs on a large wall panel to cover a number of the topics discussed in this chapter, with the title 'The Daily Life of the Soldier'. Another technique, used by the National Army Museum, the Imperial War Museum, and occasionally by other military museums, usually as part of the museum's educational service, is to have actors depicting servicemen and demonstrating some part of their drill or answering questions, in character, about service life. How successful this is depends on the extent to which the actor has been briefed. It can be a useful supplement to the static displays, and it is gaining ground as an interpretative technique in a variety of museums. It might also be claimed that military museums, by using ex-servicemen for the bulk of their staff, have people always on hand who can interpret the realities of service life for visitors, even if only for a relatively recent period.

In the final analysis it might be argued that, while the overall picture might be fairly complete, most individual regimental museums tell only a small part of the story of the life of the ordinary serviceman. Even the national museums do not tell it all. I shall return to the national museums in a later chapter, but, as far as the regimental museums are concerned, it should be remembered that they have another equally valid tale to tell, that of the achievements of their regiments, and they are only just beginning to reinterpret this in terms of the ordinary servicemen. Moreover, there would be little justification for keeping these museums open if they all concentrated on telling the same story of the daily life of their soldiers or sailors in a more or less general way. In any case most have such limited display space that concentration on every aspect of daily life would not leave any space for telling the regiment's particular story. They need to strike a balance between regimental and social history, and some could still do a lot more about introducing the story of the common man or woman into their galleries.

This brings us neatly to a consideration of the way in which women, and their fellow camp followers, are shown in military museums.

Notes

1. This seems to be generally true of European museums. Westrate (1961:6–7) points out that 'the Musée de l'Armée in Paris . . . in a very real sense . . . is a memorial to Napoleon Bonaparte'.
2. Royal Green Jackets Museum leaflet, 1994.
3. Though, ironically, the uniforms were already in the course of redesign before the outbreak of this war (letter from Colonel Peter Walton to the author, 7 February 1995).

6. Camp Followers and Specialist Units

In many military museums, women are absent, deliberately excluded by labels which assume that the word 'man' speaks for the whole population, or shown only in the role of nurse, whore or domestic servant.

(S. Wilkinson and I. Hughes 1991:24)

Most military museums concentrate, not surprisingly, on the officers and men of their own unit. They tell us very little about the many men and women who either accompanied it on its travels or lived near its barracks with the sole purpose of providing non-military services for the soldiers or sailors. Yet without this support from what can very loosely be termed the camp followers, military units could often not function efficiently, if at all.

One tends to think of women whenever the term camp follower is used. The Regiments of Gloucestershire Museum and the National Army Museum have attempted to write women back into the galleries by telling visitors about the life of an army wife. The army did not approve of marriage because it distracted the men from their duty and forced the regiments to take some responsibility for non-combatant dependents. Officers needed their Colonel's permission before they could marry, and did not, in any case, receive a marriage allowance until they were 25 years of age. Most waited until they had reached the rank of major and could afford to support a wife (Warner 1992:61). Clearly, the other ranks could not hope to reach this exalted position, and the army had to accept that some men, at least, would wish to marry during their service. Generally, therefore, a quota system was in force, which permitted six wives to be 'on the strength' for every one hundred men in the unit. These wives were allowed to live in the soldiers' accommodation, as married quarters were unknown in this period. The Regiments of Gloucestershire Museum has a display showing an army wife living with her husband in a section of a barracks divided off from the single soldiers with whom they shared the room by only a blanket, and trying to bring up a family in those conditions. The caption explains that the wife would have had to carry out some cleaning and sewing tasks for the other soldiers, as well as for her husband, in return for this meagre accommodation and for the even more meagre food ration that she received. The display clearly shows the cramped conditions and the complete lack of privacy that army wives had to endure under this scheme.

For those wives not on the strength, life could be even more difficult.

They had to live in lodgings they found for themselves, and their husband might only rarely be given permission to spend the night out of barracks. When a unit was ordered abroad, lots would be drawn amongst the women on the strength to determine which wives would be allowed to accompany the regiment, usually totalling no more than six per company. Those left behind might have to wait many years to see their husbands again, and in the meantime, until the regulations were finally changed in 1882, they received no allowances from the army and had to exist on any savings they might have, or rely on either the generosity of their family or the harsh charity of the parish. If their husband did not return, they were left to fend for themselves. Their experiences do not feature in the displays in military museums, though the Museum of the Royal Highland Fusiliers in Glasgow has a tableau of a Territorial Army soldier saying goodbye to his wife in August 1914, and the Lancashire County and Regimental Museum shows a soldier taking leave of his wife and son at the docks during the Boer War. These displays, along with some of the domestic paintings mentioned in Chapter 4, at least convey something of the heartache caused by such partings.

Life was not easy, however, for the wives who were allowed to accompany the regiment abroad or on active service. A foreign posting might mean that the wife had native servants to help her with the domestic chores, but she would have had to cope with the same hostile environment and tropical diseases which, before the emergence of modern medical techniques, decimated British troops abroad. Moreover she could become the victim of physical violence, as, for example, in the Indian Mutiny of 1857, when many British servicemen's wives were killed. She might also have had to put up with a considerable period of separation from her children, as all those who could afford to do so would send their children home to Britain for their education (Warner 1992:61). The alternative was to endure the anxiety of raising them in an alien environment. These aspects of overseas service are not usually touched on in military museums, as the picture they present of the woman's life abroad is normally conveyed by the late Victorian photographs of the Indian Raj, which show her enjoying tiffin on the lawn or tea on the verandah. The experiences of army children are rarely discussed, though they also appear in these photographic displays, such as one in the Royal Hussars Museum in Winchester, and the Regiments of Gloucestershire Museum does have a caption which discusses their education.

The experiences of women on campaign are dealt with in more detail in the National Army Museum's 'The Road to Waterloo' exhibition. Its display has a very striking life-size model of an army wife, Mrs Dan Skiddy, carrying her exhausted husband, an officer's batman with the 34th (Cumberland) Regiment of Foot, in a retreat during the Peninsular War (Figure 6.1). This and the accompanying caption make it plain that these wives undertook a number of very valuable tasks including cooking, cleaning, sewing and other domestic chores for their own husband and for the rest of his regiment, for which they were entitled to half rations. The model of the redoubtable Mrs Skiddy in the NAM shows that their contribution went beyond these domestic duties and exposed them to many of the same dangers and hardships as their men. Moreover, if their husbands were killed or died of disease, they had to marry again quickly for, as a caption in the Regimental Museum of the 9th/12th Royal Lancers Museum explains, if they were not married to another soldier within six months they were cast off the strength and could soon become destitute.

The National Army Museum caption also makes clear, though, that these women, 45,000 of whom were with the army in Spain in 1813, although brave and loyal, were not angels. They were as hard-drinking and quarrelsome as their husbands, and gave the army authorities just as many problems. Indeed Mrs Skiddy herself created consternation during one march by constantly blocking the track with the mule on

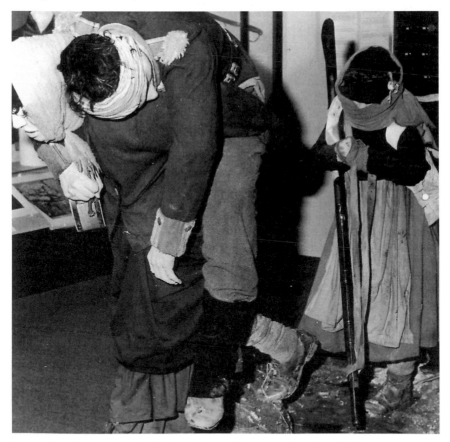

Figure 6.1 Tableau in the National Army Museum: Mrs Dan Skiddy carrying her exhausted husband during a retreat in 1812 during the Peninsular War.
Source: National Army Museum

which she was carrying her personal possessions. These women could also cause their husbands considerable difficulties. A life-size tableau in the Royal Scots Regimental Museum shows Private McBain fighting in the Battle of Malplaquet with his infant son on his back in a knapsack (Figure 6.2). His wife had decided to return home in the middle of the campaign leaving him, literally, holding the baby. But it is also obvious, as the National Army Museum makes clear, that, despite their faults, these women fulfilled a useful role.

Some of the wives acted as sutlers, which meant that they obtained and sold to the troops the extra rations the men needed to survive. This was a vital function, given the inadequacy of the supplies provided by the army commissariat service when the army was on campaign. Sutlers were also drawn, of course, from local civilians, male and female. Indeed there were 1000 Spanish and Portuguese women fulfilling this role with the army in Spain in 1813, and they were essential camp followers, though their role is unsung in military displays. Sexual services were provided by the prostitutes who have generally given camp followers a bad name, but, as we have seen, this aspect of military service is largely ignored in public displays, though references can be found to them in the diaries held in military museum archives.

Wives and other female camp followers also acted as nurses or undertakers if their men were struck down in battle or by disease. It was only during the Crimean War that Florence Nightingale pioneered the use of professional female nurses in treating the sick and wounded in foreign theatres of war, and her achievement is recorded in the museum named after her in St Thomas's Hospital in London.

Some wives and girlfriends adopted a different approach to helping their men on campaign by joining the armed forces themselves disguised as men. Folk songs from the nineteenth century refer to 'handsome cabin boys' or 'sweet young soldiers' who were in fact women in disguise who have followed their lovers into the armed forces. Genuine cases are recorded of this phenomenon and some are now celebrated in the appropriate museum. Hannah Snell, for example, followed her first husband into the army, and later served in the Royal Marines for five years. After being seriously wounded, and having to treat herself in order to avoid detection, she made her sex known to her superiors and then acted for many years as a sutler before retiring to run a public house. Her story is graphically illustrated in the Royal Marines Museum by an animated life-size model, leaning on the bar of her pub, telling her tale to a customer.

This is an interesting and unusual story, though not unique. The National Army Museum temporary display 'The Right To Serve: Women in Britain's Land Forces from the Seventeenth Century to the Present Day', which opened in November 1994, highlighted the examples of Christian Davies, known as 'Mother Ross', who enlisted in the Dragoons in 1693 in order to find her sweetheart in Flanders, and Dr James Barry, an army surgeon from 1813 until 1859, who, it was discovered on her death, was a woman. These cases indicate the bravery of such women

Figure 6.2 Tableau in the Royal Scots Regimental Museum: Private McBain fighting in the Battle of Malplaquet with his infant son in a knapsack on his back.
Source: Royal Scots Regimental Museum

and their desire for adventure. They also show, though this point is not made in the relevant displays, the poor state of personal hygiene and army medical care which allowed these women to enlist and live as men (and Hannah Snell innocently to share a bed with a man who was not her husband) for several years both on campaign and in barracks without anyone apparently suspecting their true sex. In the cases of both Hannah Snell and Christian Davies, who had very similar military experiences, it was the wounds which they received in battle which threatened exposure, not their daily round of activities.

As we have seen, these women were the exception: most women played their part behind the lines rather than in uniform, before the twentieth century. Indeed, women played a crucial and largely unrecorded part in warfare by creating and maintaining the national wealth which allowed campaigns to be planned and fought. This is alluded to in the Gurkha Museum which shows, at the beginning of its story, the important role Nepalese women play in their society (Figure 6.3), and the way in which their economic contribution through farming allows the men to leave the villages to become soldiers. But as Sue Wilkinson and Isabel Hughes (1991:26) have noted, 'at almost any period in history women have been actively involved in the business of war. They have worked in the gunmakers and armaments trade . . . they have defended their homes and castles against attack, they have tended the sick and have been the victims of rape and pillage and slaughter'. Their story deserves a bigger place than it enjoys at present in the national museums devoted to the military history of this country.

As the nineteenth century developed, armies became larger and communications improved. As a result, more notice was taken of the conditions in which soldiers lived and worked, particularly in view of their terrible suffering in the Crimean War. It became increasingly obvious that the efforts of army wives and the other unofficial camp followers were inadequate to maintain the armies in the field, and a number of specialist arms began to develop to take over these vital functions. This meant that the army wives no longer had a role to play with the regiments on campaign, and so they were left at home.

Many specialist units had been in existence for some time, of course, though their functions had been supplemented by using civilians where necessary. The Board of Ordnance, which originated in the middle of the fifteenth century, was responsible for the King's Works and Arsenals. This meant that it was answerable to the government for the royal castles and fortifications, for the artillery and for the supply of ordnance and munitions, originally to both the Royal Navy and the army. In times of war it raised a Military Train, manned by a mixture of civilian engineers and soldiers, which was tasked with conducting sieges, siting the guns, building roads and controlling munitions stores. This system was cumbersome, and, during the 1715 Jacobite rebellion, it took so long to organize a military train that the fighting was over before the guns were ready. In 1716, therefore, two companies of

Figure 6.3 Tableau in the Gurkha Museum: a Nepalese hill farmer and his wife
surrounded by their farming implements.
Source: Gurkha Museum

artillery were formed, and thus became one of the first of the specialist
units which are recognizable in the modern army. As was noted in
Chapter 2, the Royal Regiment of Artillery has a museum of guns and
equipment in the Rotunda in Woolwich, and a separate Regimental
Museum nearby which displays the men's uniforms and personal equipment and tells the history of the Royal Artillery from its formation
to the present day (though the latter museum is closed at the time of
writing).

At the same time as the Royal Artillery was formed, the Corps of Royal
Engineers also began its separate history, though, like the Royal
Artillery, it was administered by the Board of Ordnance until 1855. This

Corps has a very long pedigree, claiming its origins in the military engineers who accompanied William the Conqueror to these shores. From the middle of the fifteenth century, as we have seen, military engineers were under the control of the Board of Ordnance, and in wartime were augmented by civilians pressed into service. In 1716 a separate officer Corps of Engineers was established, and in 1787 an other-rank Corps of Military Artificers, later called the Royal Sappers and Miners, was set up. The Sappers and Miners, as their name suggests, were originally responsible for digging the ditches which could under-mine the walls of an enemy's fortification or provide protection for the gun emplacements of siege troops, while the officers of the Royal Engineers built such fortifications and were involved in surveying and building roads for military use. The two Corps were finally amalgamated in 1856. By the middle of the nineteenth century the Corps of Royal Engineers was responsible for all kinds of military building works, including construction, repairs, sewerage, water and gas supplies, and for the building of docks and numerous public buildings[1].

But building was only one part of the Royal Engineers' work. Being responsible for surveying led to map making, for which Royal Engineers had to provide sketches and illustrations, which in turn resulted in an involvement in the development of photography in its early years. The Corps of Royal Engineers also took part in experiments with balloons and man-lifting kites in the latter part of the nineteenth century, and eventually became one of the founders of military aviation. This variety of tasks undertaken by its Corps means that the Royal Engineers Museum has a wide-ranging story to tell, which it does through an extensive collection of models and pictures, as well as the normal uniform and equipment displays.

The Corps of Royal Engineers was also involved in the provision of military communications for the army until after the First World War. Good communications have always been vital in the successful conduct of military campaigns. The disaster of the Charge of the Light Brigade at Balaclava is a perfect example of the results of poor communications, but military history is full of examples of good or bad communications playing a major part in the winning or losing of particular battles. At regimental level signalling has usually been the responsibility of the regiments themselves, though their museums generally do not high-light this activity. Since the 1850s, however, signalling from regimental to brigade level and beyond has been the responsibility of a specialized unit. In the period covered by this book the unit concerned was the Royal Engineers, but in 1920 the Royal Corps of Signals was formed, and it is in its museum at Blandford that all aspects of military signalling are dealt with, from the Crimean War onwards. The museum uses visual and electrical signalling equipment, vehicles, uniforms and a collection of relics and souvenirs to tell the story of both the early military campaigns which involved the Royal Engineer signallers and those since the First World War in which the Royal Signals has played its part.

As well as good communications, a commander needs good military intelligence which can tell him what the enemy is doing and what its strengths and weaknesses are. In Ashford in Kent, the Intelligence Corps Museum uses documents, maps, photographs and uniforms to tell the story of military intelligence gathering since Elizabethan times, though the Corps itself only officially came into existence in 1912.

Army transport may seem a modern concept, and indeed most military museums concentrate on showing vehicles from the twentieth century. But supplies, men and equipment have had to be moved over all kinds of terrain since armies were first organized. Originally the army requisitioned the transport it needed, and this often included drivers from the local population. This system proved inadequate when dealing with the large armies used during the Napoleonic Wars, and a unit of Royal Waggoners was formed which became the Royal Waggon Train in 1802. The service was discontinued between 1833 and 1855, but the Crimean War again exposed the weakness of relying solely on local requisition, and the Land Transport Corps was then formed. Its eventual descendant after many changes of name and several re-organizations, the Royal Corps of Transport, had a museum in Aldershot using uniforms, pictures, dioramas and models telling the story of military transport since 1795. This Corps now forms part of the new Royal Logistic Corps, and its collection has moved to Camberley. Some of the original vehicles from this period, together with an impressive collection of more modern military transport of all kinds, can be seen in the Museum of Army Transport at Beverley, an independent museum partly supported by the local authority.

Most of this early transport was pulled by horses. In the seventeenth and eighteenth centuries the care of army horses was entrusted to farriers, but from the end of the eighteenth century regiments began to appoint veterinary surgeons. In 1858 the Veterinary Medical Department was formed and later reorganized as the Army Veterinary Department. In 1903 an Army Veterinary Corps, composed of other ranks only, was formed, and amalgamated with the Army Veterinary Department in 1906 to form the Royal Army Veterinary Corps. Aldershot used to be the home of the Royal Army Veterinary Corps Museum, whose collection contains material relating to the work of army veterinary surgeons since the middle of the nineteenth century, but which is, at the time of writing, closed pending relocation.

These were all important specialist units at the strategic level, but equally important changes took place in the army's organization which affected the common soldier more directly. As has been noted, wives constituted an important part of the medical and nursing services provided for the troops on campaign before the late nineteenth century. They could not, of course, cater for all the medical needs of the men, nor did wives serve on ships to be on hand to nurse sick sailors. The services of trained medical men were needed, therefore, to tend the men when in port or in barracks, and to accompany them on board ship and on campaign. As a result, trained surgeons were made available to the armed forces from the seventeenth century onwards.

Army surgeons were originally provided on a regimental basis, though their numbers were never adequate, and many units had to make do with the services of poorly trained orderlies. This system, as was only too painfully obvious at the time, broke down during the Crimean War, and in 1855 a Medical Staff Corps was formed. The Royal Army Medical Corps, formed in 1898, is the direct descendant of the army surgeons and the men of the Medical Staff Corps, and has its museum in Aldershot where an account of its work, and that of its predecessors from Tudor times, is given. The Royal Army Medical Corps Historical Museum displays an interesting collection of surgeons' instruments from various periods, including some unusual items like the Longmore Bullet Extractor, and the home-made 'coin catcher' from the Boer War used to extract halfpenny coins from the gullets of soldiers who had swallowed them in an attempt to avoid the firing line. It also contains examples of army surgeons' uniforms and an impressive display of medals, including panels recounting the stories behind the many VCs won by them, as well as some exotic souvenirs and the personal effects of leading members of the corps. But perhaps the most interesting items are the series of watercolours, painted by a surgeon, Sir Charles Bell, which show in graphic detail the wounds suffered by some of the casualties at the Battle of Waterloo, and the numerous other exhibits in the museum demonstrating the effects of weapons on human flesh and bone. These displays help to provide the grim reminder of the realities of armed conflict which, as I argued in Chapter 4, is usually missing from military museum displays.

Army nursing also became a separate and professional occupation after the Crimean War. Trained nurses, both male and female, gradually replaced the untrained orderlies and the amateurs. The Army Nursing Service was formed in 1881, to be supplemented in wartime by the Army Nursing Reserve established in 1897. In 1902 the service was reorganized and named the Queen Alexandra's Imperial Military Nursing Service. Its achievements are celebrated in the Queen Alexandra's Royal Army Nursing Corps Museum, also in Aldershot, through photographs, pictures, uniforms, medals and relics such as the Communion set purchased by Florence Nightingale for the soldiers in Scutari Hospital.

The medical theme is completed by another Aldershot museum, the Royal Army Dental Corps Historical Museum. The Royal Army Dental Corps was formed in 1921, but its museum tells the story of army dentistry from 1660 to the present day through a collection of uniforms, medals, photographs and early dental instruments.

The Red Cross, which has played such a major part in succouring the wounded and prisoners of war since it was formed in the middle of the nineteenth century, is an international organization. The British Red Cross has a public museum in Guildford which holds a collection of early medical and nursing equipment, uniforms, medals and memorabilia illustrating its activities since 1859. Its work is also recorded in the First and Second World War displays of most regimental museums.

The spiritual needs of the army were well cared for during the English Civil War when every regiment had a chaplain. But by the late eighteenth century many of these regimental chaplains were in the habit of appointing poorly trained deputies to undertake their duties, and some units, especially when on active service, were very badly served. Finally, in 1796, regimental chaplains were abolished and the Army Chaplains Department came into being. The army chaplains have their museum in Bagshot in Surrey, though its exhibits are mainly from the twentieth century.

Education was an aspect of life not considered very highly by the military authorities until the nineteenth century. Men were trained to undertake their military tasks through repetition and harsh discipline. They were not educated. The increasing complexity of weapons and tactics in the nineteenth century, however, showed that soldiers needed to be more flexible and more adaptable, which meant better educated. This led in 1846 to the formation of the Corps of Army Schoolmasters, which later became the Royal Army Educational Corps. Its museum in Beaconsfield shows, through a collection of badges, buttons, photographs and documents, the growth of army education since 1815, and illustrates in particular the work of the Corps in India, Africa and the Far East. The work of army schoolmistresses, who were recruited in the 1860s to work in the Army's infant and industrial schools, was recorded in the National Army Museum's 'The Right to Serve' exhibition.

Physical training in the army was formalized a little later than army education. The Army Gymnastic Staff, later called the Army Physical Training Corps, was set up in 1860 and the small Army Physical Training Corps Museum in Aldershot concentrates, through the use of photographs, documents, uniforms, medals, gymnastic equipment and sports apparatus, on the theme of the soldier-sportsman since that date.

Army pay was looked after by regimental paymasters until the Army Pay Department was formed in 1878 and the Army Pay Corps in 1899. This corps had its own museum at Winchester dealing with its work in the twentieth century, though it is temporarily closed at the time of writing awaiting relocation. The much maligned Army Catering Corps now forms part of the Royal Logistic Corps and no longer has a separate museum.

New uniforms were supplied originally by the unit commander, though this was eventually a function of the commissariat, and later still of the predecessor of the Royal Army Ordnance Corps, which is also now part of the Royal Logistic Corps. Its collection shares the new Royal Logistic Corps Museum at Blackdown, near Camberley, with those of the Royal Corps of Transport, the Army Catering Corps and the Royal Pioneer Corps. Uniforms had to be repaired, of course, and this was often a job undertaken by wives, or by soldiers using their 'housewife' kits of needles and thread. More important or more major repairs and renovations would have been carried out by skilled tailors, and a life-sized tableau in the Regiments of Gloucestershire Museum shows a scene outside a regimental tailor's tent at the Royal Gloucestershire

Hussars' Annual Camp in 1908, with the tailor at work and a customer showing off the dress uniform he has just had repaired.

All regiments had their own musicians, even if only a drummer and a fife player to beat time for the march or to signal. During the late eighteenth and early nineteenth centuries a number of military bands were formed, which played during parades and on ceremonial occasions and provided musicians for Officers' Mess dances and parties. They quickly became an accepted part of the military and civilian scene in Britain and in her colonies. Most regiments and corps pay tribute in their museums to their musicians by displaying examples of their instruments, uniforms, and sheet music and by hanging paintings of their bands on the walls. The Royal Marines Museum, for example, devotes a small side gallery to the history of its world-renowned band, and the Guards Museum has a smaller but similar display on its bands. The Royal Military School of Music at Kneller Hall, where military musicians are trained, has its own small museum of musical instruments since 1780 and appropriate sheet music. The potential of all this music is perhaps best realized by the Guards Museum which regales its visitors with a constant recital of recorded martial and popular tunes from the Guards' massed bands.

Other specialist corps and services grew up in the late nineteenth and early twentieth centuries to take over or augment some specialist function previously carried out as one of the many duties of the squaddy, or by civilian contractors. Though most of their displays fall outside the scope of this work, there are museums catering, for example, for the Corps of Military Police in Chichester and the Royal Electrical and Mechanical Engineers at Arborfield. All these specialist corps and their antecedent units played a vital, but often unsung, part in the maintenance of the British Army and in the successes it achieved, as well as, on occasion, in its failures.

On the whole the Royal Navy does not have separate museums for its specialists. There are, of course, the Royal Navy Submarine Museum at Gosport and the Fleet Air Arm Museum at Yeovilton. These are important museums but, like the Tank Museum at Bovington Camp, the Airborne Forces Museum at Aldershot, the Museum of Army Flying at Middle Wallop and the RAF Museum at Hendon, the bulk of their collections and the story which they have to tell lie outside the period covered by this book.

The functions of most other naval specialists are dealt with in the exhibitions in the National Maritime Museum and in the Royal Naval Museum. Throughout both these museums there are exhibits relating to navigation, naval gunnery, chart making and other specialisms that naval officers were presumed to have at their command. The sailor was also expected, as the Royal Naval Museum points out, to be a jack of all trades, though its 'HMS Victory and the Campaign of Trafalgar' gallery shows through tableaux, prints and collections of artifacts that there were specialists, who included carpenters, cooks and gunners, on board naval ships. Naval signalling, for example, was (and is) a very specialized practice. Before the advent of radio, communicating between ships at sea and between ships and the land required men trained in the use of visual signalling systems using flags, semaphore machines or lights. This equipment and the systems of codes used with it are very well explained in a small display at the National Maritime Museum in the 'The Way of a Ship' gallery, where various other specialist functions required in sailing naval ships are also examined.

The Royal Naval Museum discusses the way in which these specialist tasks developed in the age of steam, and how others, relating to the new engines, were introduced. It also explains that many non-military tasks were originally carried out by specially appointed warrant officers, but that, in the later Victorian era, these became commissioned officers, and specialist branches grew up to deal with these tasks. It has display cases on The Paymaster, The Medical Officer, and The Navigator, as examples of such branches. At the same time there are panels describing the development of the Royal Naval Gunnery School in the 1830s in which the ordinary sailors, for the first time, were given organized specialist training.

There is, of course, one specialist naval museum which comes within the terms of reference of this book, that of the Royal Marines. The Royal Marines were originally raised as 'sea soldiers' in 1664, though they were only formed in times of crisis, and disbanded when peace returned, during the first 90 years of their history. In 1755, 50 Companies of Marines were raised to serve under the Admiralty during the Seven Years War, and the Royal Marines have served continuously as both infantry and artillery on land and in naval ships ever since. The Royal Marines Museum was founded in 1958, and in 1975 its collection was arranged in its present home in the former Officers' Mess at Eastney Barracks in Portsmouth (figure 6.4). It has its own unique story to tell, but, in view of the military function of this corps, its museum more closely resembles that of an army regiment than that of either of the naval museums examined here.

This is also, perhaps, an appropriate place to consider some of the other units which played an important part in the military history of this country during the relevant period, but which do not find a place in most military museums. In the eighteenth century, for example, shortages in the number of troops available to the monarch in times of war were overcome by the hiring of mercenaries. Hanoverian and other German troops played a leading role in Britain's army during the Seven Years War, the American Revolutionary War and the Napoleonic Wars. The National Army Museum has two life-sized models, one of a private in De Roll's (Swiss) Regiment serving in Malta in 1800, and the other an Officer in the 2nd Dragoons, King's German Legion, in Spain in 1813, which demonstrate this foreign mercenary presence in the British Army of the period. The most famous of the foreign mercenary forces used by the British, the Gurkhas, have, of course, their own museum in Winchester which commemorates their service with the British Army since 1815.

Figure 6.4 The Royal Marines Museum in Eastney Barracks with its external exhibits.
Source: Peter Thwaites

The Gurkha regiments were originally part of the Imperial Indian Army, and the history and artifacts of that huge force are looked after by the National Army Museum. In its 'The Victorian Soldier' gallery is a model of an Indian soldier of the 53rd Bengal Native Infantry and his wife. Nearby are uniforms of the East India Company and the Indian Army, as well as a number of artifacts relating to the British in India and to Indian troops. Another display relating to these forces can be seen in the Indian Army Memorial Room, which is part of the National Army Museum Sandhurst Departments at the Royal Military Academy Sandhurst.

The National Army Museum also has a model of a Fellah from the Sudanese Battalion, shown near Omderman in 1898, and a model of a Queensland Mounted Infantry soldier during the Boer War, as tributes to the many other imperial troops who fought beside the British Army during the conflicts of the nineteenth and twentieth centuries.

The story of camp followers and specialists would not be complete, however, without considering some of God's other creatures which play a part in military life. We tend, of course, to think of camp followers as being invariably human. But a visit to a military barracks or camp today will soon reveal a large number of non-human residents. Dogs, for example, seem to play a large part in the lives of servicemen and their families. Not only are they to be seen in the quarters, but dogs often accompany their owners to work in military offices.

It is hardly surprising, therefore, that dogs feature in military museum displays, particularly as the British serviceman seems adept at making friends with foreign animals. Bobbie, for example, who was befriended by soldiers during the Afghan campaign in 1880, now stares out through glass eyes at visitors to the Museum of the Duke of Edinburgh's Royal Regiment, while Nell, an Egyptian dog, sits in a glass case in the Royal Marines Museum. Nell, who adopted a Royal Marine Artillery Battery in Alexandria in 1882, was awarded Egyptian Campaign medals, and these and her gravestone are also on display in the museum.

The British love of animals extends beyond dogs, of course, to include a surprising variety of creatures. The National Army Museum, for example, has on display Crimean Tom, a cat adopted by an officer of the 6th Dragoons at Sebastapol during the Crimean War, and the Aldershot Military Museum boasts the gravestone of a pet lioness. Jacob the goose, whose head is lovingly preserved in the Guards Museum, was the unit pet of the 2nd Battalion of the Coldstream Guards in Canada and warned the British soldiers of the approach of French rebels in 1838.

Other animals achieve a status beyond mere pets and become unit mascots. A number of British regiments have dogs, goats or ponies as mascots which lead their parades while they are alive and whose images grace their unit museums after their death.

But not all animals were treated in such a sentimental way by the army. Animals provided a number of different services for the army both at home and overseas. The Royal Signals Museum has a stuffed pigeon, which was one of the heroes of the message-carrying pigeon service, and photographs on display and in its archive show that dogs, camels, mules, horses and even elephants were used in the late nineteenth century for laying telegraph wire for advancing troops during foreign campaigns.

It is, however, as beasts of burden that animals feature most often in military museums. The Royal Signals Museum exhibits a cable wagon, first used in 1907, which would have needed eight horses to operate it. Military carts can be seen in the Museum of Army Transport, and as models in various other museums, and would have been pulled by horses, mules or oxen. The Museum of Artillery shows that its guns could not have been brought into action, even as late as the First World War, without these draft animals. Indeed until this century no British army could campaign without the motive power supplied by these beasts of burden.

Commanders also relied on their mounts to give them the mobility they needed to keep in touch with their troops. Napoleon's charger, Marengo, was captured after the Battle of Waterloo by Lord Petre, and its skeleton now forms part of 'The Road To Waterloo' exhibition in the National Army Museum.

But horses played a much more important role than merely giving mobility to the commander and his senior officers. Troops mounted on horses have long been a major arm of the British Army, though true cavalry units, which relied on the speed and power of the horse to give them their effectiveness, only date from the middle of the seventeenth century. Cavalry museums, like the Royal Hussars Museum at Winchester, contain a number of paintings showing the horse in battle, as well as models of these cavalry horses and their riders in all their finery.

These horses had to be looked after, of course, and it was a chore that took up much of the time of cavalry soldiers, and indeed of all mounted units. Both the Regimental Museum of the Queen's Own Hussars (Figure 6.5) and the Regimental Museum of the 9th/12th Royal Lancers have very good tableaux showing horses being tended by soldiers in their stables, and the 9th/12th Royal Lancers' Museum has captions which explain how horses were acquired by the army, and the different types which were found suitable as mounts when cavalry tactics changed and developed in the nineteenth century.

Less noble creatures than the horse can also be counted as camp followers, though they appear less often in museum displays. Perhaps

Figure 6.5 Stable scene from the Regimental Museum of the Queen's Own Hussars: the Regimental Barracks at Hounslow preparing for the visit of HRH the Duke of Connaught in 1885.
Source: Regimental Museum of the Queen's Own Hussars

the most obvious is the rat, which would always have been on hand to share the soldiers' and sailors' rations. Rats do appear in the mock First World War trenches which can be seen in both the Imperial War Museum and the Museum of the Manchesters, amongst others, but they rarely seem to feature in earlier displays. Also largely absent are the fleas, lice and insects which feature so largely in personal accounts of life on campaign, though 22 of these less than noble creatures appear in a set of glass jars in the Royal Norfolk Regimental Museum, where they are described as 'specimens of the other enemies which confront soldiers on active service in tropical climes'. A display in the Royal Marines Museum shows the weevils which infested food on board naval ships. Otherwise mention of such animals is relegated to the guide books and archives in other military museums.

But perhaps we should use the noble horse as the exemplar of the animal camp follower rather than the flea. The horse has, after all, a special place in military history, and is often used to symbolize the martial spirit. In the next chapter, the yeomanry, the volunteer cavalry of the British Isles, are featured as part of an examination of the way the interrelationship between civil society and the armed forces in the period under review is dealt with in museums.

Notes

1. Including the Science Museum in South Kensington and the Albert Hall.

7. The Military in the Domestic Setting

The problem of civil-military relationships is one with which . . . all societies have to deal.

(M. Howard 1959:12)

The armed forces do not exist in a vacuum. They are recruited from, paid for and ultimately controlled by the civilian population. Yet the interrelationship between these two sides of the same population is a complex one. In the Royal Naval Museum there is an interesting display, called 'Images of the Sailor', which looks at the public image of the ordinary sailor of the Royal Navy over the last two hundred years. It seems that, after an unfortunate period in the eighteenth century when sailors were usually represented in songs and stories as foul-mouthed ruffians, matelots were invariably portrayed in cartoons, paintings, books, popular songs, and later in films, as attractive, cheerful, brave and trustworthy. Jolly Jack Tar was, in fact, a generally popular fellow who achieved heroic status during the early Victorian era when naval ships were keeping the arteries of the empire open. This was in marked contrast to the popular image of the soldier at the same time who was generally represented as a licentious, drunken and savage beast. Rudyard Kipling succinctly summed up the popular prejudice against the soldier in his poem 'Tommy Atkins', while the sailor is epitomized in the laudatory song 'Hearts of Oak'. This difference in popularity was to diminish by the end of the nineteenth century, when the newspapers became full of reports of the achievements of brave soldiers in battles against the Queen's enemies in far-off lands. Nevertheless, popular prejudice against the army had been a feature of British domestic life for 200 years.

The popularity of the sailor may be explained, at least in part, by the fact that the navy operated away from these shores throughout this period and therefore only the coastal towns ever saw sailors in any numbers. We are living in an age when the army is similarly more or less invisible. Today, soldiers are shown on television fighting in the Gulf or providing humanitarian aid in Bosnia. But most civilians only see soldiers in the flesh when following a military convoy on the motorway, or when they attend a military tattoo. Soldiers off duty invariably wear civilian clothes and try to melt into the background. Since the Second World War, only in Northern Ireland have armed British soldiers been seen on the streets of British towns.

This was not true of the period covered by this study. Soldiers were a common sight, in their bright and distinctive uniforms, in many towns and cities throughout the kingdom. When they swaggered down the street, got involved in drunken brawls or insulted young ladies, they were much more in the public eye than their sailor comrades, who, it must be said, were probably acting just as badly several thousand miles away in some foreign port.

But the public dislike and distrust of the army had deeper causes than just the high profile and low moral standing of many of its soldiers (see Barnett 1970:169). As a caption in the Lancashire County and Regimental Museum explains, its roots lay instead in both the potential threat a standing army was thought to pose to civil liberties and the considerable burden the cost of maintaining this army imposed on all taxpayers. The attempt made by King Charles I to use the army to force his will on Parliament, and the virtual military dictatorship which had followed the Civil War, alerted people to the apparent danger that the army might be employed as a repressive arm of government. This fear was reinforced both by the actions of King James II, who built up a standing army between 1685 and 1688 which he seemed ready to turn on his own people, and by the more blatant examples of other European monarchs of the seventeenth and eighteenth centuries who used their armies to oppress their subjects. As a result, the Declaration of Rights of 1688 stated that it was illegal to maintain a standing army in peacetime without the consent of Parliament, and the Act of Settlement of 1689 made the very existence of the army subject to the annual passing of an Act of Parliament. After most wars of the eighteenth and nineteenth centuries the army was, therefore, cut severely, its numbers dropping, for example, from 200,000 at the end of Marlborough's campaigns to just 12,000 by 1719. This, then, made it ill-prepared to face the next confrontation. But, as the military historian Michael Howard has observed, 'The conflict between liberty and authority obsessed the thinkers of the 17th and 18th centuries, and for them the question of the control of the armed forces was central and inescapable' (1959:21). The purchase system, for example, whereby army officers bought their original commissions and each subsequent promotion, for all its obvious anomalies, was preserved because it was believed that it prevented the formation of an officer caste separate from the rest of the nation, with its own agenda and loyalties.

This fear of and hostility towards the army was compounded by it being employed by the government as a proto-police force. Before the formation of police forces in the middle of the nineteenth century, local law enforcement was weak and relied on the voluntary support of the local population. It was unable to cope with the mass demonstrations or riots which might break out in times of economic depression or during contested parliamentary elections. At such moments the army would be called in to put down the disturbances. Occasionally, troops might be sent into a constituency before the election took place, if the government or local authorities thought that the parliamentary contest could lead to a breach of peace. Clearly, at such times the troops would have appeared to represent a real threat to the liberties of the people or to the government's political opponents.

The Regimental Museum of the 9th/12th Royal Lancers points out that soldiers were also used to enforce the unpopular Revenue Acts, which imposed duties on a range of imported luxury goods, by combating smuggling. This meant that soldiers had to be billeted in coastal areas to attack a trade in foreign wines, spirits and other commodities which was a popular and profitable sideline for people from all ranks of society. It is little wonder that soldiers were so unpopular in comparison to their sailor colleagues, who would have been an inefficient tool for the suppression of civil liberties, were rarely used as police, and whose anti-smuggling activities usually took place at sea, well away from popular gaze.

The public perception of the army, however, did change very slowly. In the first place, royal control over the army weakened between 1689 and 1714 because of the growth of the power of government ministers. This removed the threat of the arbitrary use of military power by the monarch, though obviously the danger that the elected government could employ this force against its opponents remained. The growing civil control of the army is indeed a complex and interesting topic which is not dealt with in any detail in British military museums, though it must be admitted that it is not a subject which lends itself easily to representation in a museum display. Perhaps we need a museum of government that can show this increasing political control of the armed forces as part of the general growth of parliamentary government which took place during this period.

The second major factor in altering public perceptions was the imperial expansion from the middle of the eighteenth century, which created an obvious need for a standing army to defend Britain's interests in these far-off colonies. In the past there had always been those who had claimed that Britain did not need a standing army while it was safe behind the shield of its navy, and had a militia ready to defend its shores against invasion. Arguably it had never, in fact, been possible for Britain to stand aside totally from European involvement and rely on a 'blue-water' strategy, but this was now clearly irrelevant when there were these far outposts of empire to hold and protect. The navy could keep the sea lanes open and try to prevent rival powers from capturing the colonies, but these outposts would have to be held and defended by troops on the ground (see Barnett 1970:131,188).

Finally, in 1829, a police force was formed in London, to be followed within a few years by similar forces throughout the country. This meant that the army's policing role declined, and by the middle of the century it had virtually ceased; though as the Guards Museum's 1994 exhibition, 'As safe as the Bank of England', showed it was to continue defending the Bank against possible civil disturbance for another 150 years. But the army had ceased to be an obvious threat to civil liberties. There was indeed, by the middle of the nineteenth century, a larger standing army than ever before, but up to two-thirds of it was permanently stationed overseas, which meant that it was much less in evidence on British streets, and it was no longer being used, as a matter of course, to break up civil disturbances or oversee elections.

Yet it would be a mistake to assume that this meant that the army had become universally popular overnight. There had always been another powerful strand to the opposition to a standing army: cost. It is indeed virtually impossible to disentangle the arguments for disbanding the standing army in peacetime, because of the threat to civil liberties, from those concerned with the unwarranted cost of maintaining such an expensive force any longer than was necessary. In wartime the cost of the armed forces was a tremendous burden on the taxpayers (Barnett 1970:213), and citizens understandably sought relief from this in times of peace. The navy usually fared better than the army when these peacetime cuts were made, because of the importance attached by the government to defending British shores and British trade. Then, as has been said earlier in this chapter, as the empire grew, the need to maintain a standing army, as well as a navy, in peace-time became more widely accepted. But, as a result, there were always those, like the free-traders Richard Cobden and John Bright, who opposed the retention or expansion of the empire mainly because of the financial burden, which included the cost of a large army and navy, that it imposed on the many for the apparent benefit of the few (Howard 1978:42–3). Similar arguments about the cost of maintaining the armed forces are, indeed, still being heard today, but they are rarely discussed in military museums.

Kenneth Hudson (1991:17) has also noted that it is still very difficult to find a military museum in Europe, or anywhere in the world, which says anything about the cost of wars. He would like to see a selection of guns and uniforms with a price-tag fixed to them and compared with the weekly wage at the time. As we have already seen, WHAM have called for a greater emphasis in military history displays on the part played by women, and we might add civilian men, not only in working in the industries which support military action, but also in producing the wealth that pays for it (Wilkinson and Hughes 1991:26).

It could be argued that these overarching topics are not suitable for discussion in the regimental museums, but it is perhaps surprising that they are not tackled to any great extent in the national museums' displays. Perhaps, as Dennis Oomen (1992:49) has argued in reply to Kenneth Hudson, these topics could just as easily be dealt with by museums whose collections are based on social and economic themes, by mounting exhibitions which interpret the impact of warfare in these areas. This may be another example of where a national social history museum might have a part to play in telling our national story.

Such displays would have to present a balanced picture by putting a price-tag on the trading benefits which accrued to this country by these wars or through the use of these armed forces. It was, after all, the Royal Navy which kept the trade arteries of this country open, while the army held the rich colonies like India and South Africa and beat off economic and political rivals such as France and Spain, or overcame internal revolts. As Michael Howard has pointed out (Howard 1976:48) 'merchants saw state power, especially naval power, as a necessary means of increasing their commerce'. Displays in the National Maritime Museum and the Royal Naval Museum show the work of the navy in keeping the sea lanes open, while regimental museums demonstrate the involvement of their units in the various colonial campaigns and in the occupation of these colonies. But none of these displays really explains the importance of these activities to the economy of this country in those years.

Nor do they discuss the way in which British politicians, particularly in the nineteenth century, used these forces, or the threat of them, to exert an unparalleled influence in world affairs, without endangering the well-being of the general public. As Correlli Barnett (1970:273) has said, 'Thanks to their (professional) army, the British people as a whole never felt the burdens of world power during the Victorian age', yet at the same time the army 'permitted the creation of the mental climate where the British were ready to project their own sense of law and civic docility into the jungle of international rivalry'. These are all aspects of the military history of this nation which need to be discussed, but which do not find a place in regimental, corps or naval museums because they were of no concern to individual units, who accepted the motto 'Theirs not to reason why, theirs but to do and die'.

There seems to be less reason, though, why regimental museums and local museums with military collections cannot tackle the local domestic impact of the armed forces on people's lives. Before the 1790s the army did not use barracks, and soldiers were quartered in 'inns, livery stables, ale-houses, victualling houses and all houses selling brandy, strong-waters, cider or metheglin to be drunk on the premises' (Barnett 1970:143), and occasionally in private houses, though under the Declaration of Rights no soldier could be billeted on a private householder without the householder's consent. These soldiers were fed and housed by their reluctant landlord, who was unlikely to feel he had been adequately paid for the inconvenience. It made the army very unpopular, especially as these unwelcome lodgers were not always well-behaved, having been, as Correlli Barnett (1970:169) reminds us, 'recruited from wastrels and delinquents', and with little to do once their day's duty was over but drink the strong liquor the landlord might sell them in order to gain some profit from having them under his roof. For their part the soldiers had to put up with whatever standard of food and accommodation their unwilling host provided. This unhappy relationship ended with the building of barracks, but even then soldiers remained a drain on local resources.

Before the middle of the nineteenth century, for example, the army did not have its own transport, and would have to impress beasts of burden and waggons from local authorities whenever a unit needed to move location or carry out manoeuvres (Barnett 1970:213), and having a regiment moving through a district usually meant that local traders would have to supply it with food for its men and fodder for the animals, for which sufficient recompense might not always be forthcoming.

But the drain on local resources can be seen to go beyond the more obvious taxes, costs and impositions. The armed forces, for example, had to obtain their recruits from somewhere. It is quite understandable, in a period before good communications and public transport, that, on the whole, men would only travel short distances to join up. Moreover, it was only with the expansion of the army into a number of specialist corps in the late nineteenth century that most men had a real choice in the type of service they wanted to join, and could look beyond their local infantry regiment. Traditionally, therefore, regiments recruited from the area around their depot garrison or from wherever they were stationed when new recruits were needed, while sailors were generally recruited or pressed from among the seamen found near most naval bases.

This local relationship is particularly emphasized in the Regiments of Gloucestershire Museum. There, in the entrance to the museum, an animated figure, sitting in what is apparently the snug bar of a local pub, dressed in his Victorian Gloucestershire Regiment uniform, welcomes you to the museum and points out that the two regiments dealt with in the museum (the other being the Royal Gloucestershire Hussars) were locally recruited regiments, and that visitors (assuming that they are from the local area) will be learning about the history of their relatives.

The Museum of the Manchesters, as we shall see later, makes a similar point. In fact many regimental museums make this connection between the regiment and the local people from whom their recruits came. The Military Museum of Devon and Dorset, for example, as has already been noted, emphasizes the relationship between the social history of its soldiers and that of the farm hands from whom they would have been drawn and aims at displaying the whole military heritage of the two counties and not just that of their regular army regiments.

What is not shown so clearly in military museums, however, is the effect this recruiting would have had on local families and on the local economy. Rioting accompanied the activities of some of the eighteenth-century recruiting parties and press gangs as the populace reacted violently to the prospect of their young men being taken away. Such disturbances are rarely mentioned in museum displays; neither is the economic effect on the young recruits' family, who had been deprived in this way of a breadwinner, examined. As we have seen, moreover, the soldier too badly wounded to carry out a civilian trade and the serviceman's widow were both likely to become a drain on their family, or on the local poor relief, before improvements in the pensions scheme introduced in the late nineteenth century moved the burden onto the state.

There was, of course, another side of this coin. As the Regiments of Gloucestershire Museum points out, men often joined the army in times of economic hardship. The armed forces could then be said to have been providing a form of out-relief and helping to take unemployed, and perhaps even unemployable, people off the poor relief rolls. It is an aspect of the military/civilian relationship which might warrant more attention, perhaps in the national museums, or, as Oomen (1992:49) seems to suggest, in local history museums, though, as the example of the Museum of the Manchesters will indicate, such topics could be given more attention in regimental museums as well.

Moreover, it should be remembered that the armed forces were also major employers of civilian labour: indeed for several centuries the Royal Navy was Britain's largest employer. Chapter 6 has shown that civilians followed the army on campaign and provided services or furnished supplies. These functions also had to be duplicated around home depots. Soldiers still had to be fed, clothed and entertained, and naval ships had to be supplied and their crews provided for. These wants were met by civilian contractors, local tradesmen and tradeswomen, and by local craftsmen. Payment for these goods and services brought much needed money into local economies. The armed forces also required specialized goods such as guns, ships and other weapons of war, which helped to establish major industries in Birmingham, Sheffield and other cities and to stimulate some aspects of the industrial revolution, particularly the developments in metallurgy and the production of chemicals.

Some idea of the importance of the armed forces as an employer of civilian labour and as a stimulator of industry can be gleaned from the Historic Dockyard at Chatham in Kent. Although not strictly a *military* museum, this complex records the 400-year history of this Royal Dockyard, during which time it provided Britain with over 400 warships, including HMS *Victory*. The 80-acre site, which has been turned into a working museum, tells the story of the lives and work of the carpenters and other craftsmen who built these ships, and also shows the impact of the dockyard on the local area. Similar museum and heritage complexes are planned for the Woolwich Arsenal and for the site of the Royal Gunpowder Factory in Waltham Abbey (*Museums Journal* 1994, 3:12). They will help to demonstrate the economic interrelationship between the armed forces and their civilian servants and masters.

It should also be noted, of course, that not all soldiers were looked on with fear and loathing. The Royal Engineers, perhaps uniquely, have had a history of mutually beneficial interaction with the civil authorities and the civilian population of the areas in which they have served. Indeed the Royal Engineers Museum considers that 'the third distinct strand in the story (of the Royal Engineers) is the world-wide work of the Corps in civil engineering, architecture and survey'[1], which has left behind a collection of noble public buildings, as well as a number of docks and prisons, both in Britain and throughout the Commonwealth. But the Royal Engineers' involvement in communications also made a positive contribution to nineteenth-century civilian life in Britain. In the 1870s the government took over the numerous inefficient telegraph companies which had been attempting to provide a public service, and established instead the telegraphic section of the GPO. It was the Royal Engineers Telegraph Companies, as the Royal Signals Museum explains, which set up the new system, and thereby helped to revolutionize public communications.

The Royal Army Medical Corps Historical Museum also shows, through numerous examples, that army surgeons were at the forefront, in the late nineteenth century, of research into cures for the major tropical diseases. It cost lives, and is another example of the army working in the non-military field for the good of both the civilian and military communities. It must be admitted, however, that such positive interactions were unusual before the twentieth century.

British military history is by no means exclusively the province of the regular professional military forces. The arguments about the need for a standing army partly revolved, as we have seen, around the ability of the militia to provide local defence. This was a traditional force, raised by ballot from local people and intended for purely local defence in times of emergency, after which it would be stood down. It was believed to be a far safer option than a standing army, because 'it was the nation in arms and not unquestionably obedient to the king' (Barnett 1970:116). It was also far cheaper to maintain. Unfortunately it proved to be a very inefficient military weapon. After the restoration of King Charles II in 1660 it became a part-time force; Charles and his successors generally relied for their defence on the small standing army allowed them by Parliament. As a result the militia was not called upon for active service between 1715 and 1745, and was then found to be in a very sorry state. This led to the 1757 Militia Act which took the management of this force away from the local gentry and placed it into the hands of local government (Cousins 1968). After a further 120 years of mixed fortunes, control of the militia passed to the War Office, and in 1881 militia regiments became battalions of the newly formed county regiments. But the militia virtually disappeared in 1907, and today the Royal Monmouthshire Royal Engineers (Militia) Museum displays the historical artifacts of its sole surviving regiment, while the other militia units are usually remembered in the relevant regimental or local history museums.

The Militia Act was unpopular because the rich could often gain exemption, and men disliked the element of compulsion. On the other hand, there were large numbers of men who were ready and willing to serve their country in its defence but who did not wish to enlist in the regular forces for life. As early as 1649 companies of volunteers had been formed, and in 1758 militia units were given permission to accept volunteers. By 1778 these volunteers were being formed into separate companies, and constituted half the total strength of the militia.

The spectre of invasion raised by the French Revolutionary and Napoleonic Wars led to the setting up of separate Armed Associations of Volunteers, and to the strengthening of the volunteer cavalry units, the yeomanry, which began forming in 1794. This volunteer force reached 200,000 members during these wars but was largely disbanded when they ended.

The yeomanry units, however, which were made up of the well-to-do local gentry, often using the motto 'Liberty, Loyalty and Property' which reflected their political orientation, survived this general disbandment and were supplemented in the 1830s by volunteer infantry units. Both were used to assist the regular army in civil disturbances which resulted from the struggle for the franchise. This role diminished in the middle of the nineteenth century with the formation of the civilian police forces. Then, worsening relations with France led to a revival of volunteer units in both the army and navy, and this time they became permanently established. These units received a tremendous moral boost at the end of the century, when 26,000 volunteers served alongside regular troops in South Africa during the Boer War and were seen to be a valuable addition to the force.

By 1907 the volunteer units were under strength and badly equipped. As part of a general review of the nation's armed forces, Lord Haldane replaced the old volunteer units and militia regiments with a new Territorial Force which more closely followed the pattern and training of the regular forces. It was to be able to act either as a Home Defence Force or as a supplement to a British Expeditionary Force, and it played this latter role successfully in the First World War.

The volunteer forces therefore had a chequered career in the nineteenth century, being stood down in times of peace and revived in the face of civil strife or the threat of foreign invasion. They always seemed able to attract a substantial number of men (and later women) willing to give up their spare time and spend their own money on equipment in order to defend their country and to enjoy, if for only a limited time, the military life (see Cousins 1968).

As these part-time soldiers lived within both worlds, it is appropriate, therefore, that they are remembered in both local authority museums and in regimental museums. The direct descendants of these volunteer army regiments are today's Territorial Army (TA) units, many of whom still bear the names of these older yeomanry or infantry formations; some TA Halls contain such volunteer regiment museums. The Fusiliers (City of London) Volunteer and Territorial Museum, for example, is situated in a TA hall in Balham in London, while the Hereford Light Infantry Museum and the Westminster Dragoons Museum are also sited in local TA centres. All in all some 20 TA centres hold volunteer force museums, though cutbacks are making them increasingly rare. In any case, they are only allowed to occupy rooms in the TA centres on the basis 'that they are using space surplus to other requirements, or sharing space used for another primary purpose ... and that they do not add to the running costs of the TA Centre' (MGC 1990:25). They have no official funding, which means that they cannot employ a full-time curator, and any money that they spend on the display or care of the collections must come from donations or regimental funds. Not surprisingly their facilities are generally on the poor side, and they are usually not open to the public. More and more of these museums are being absorbed either into the museum of their parent regular army regiment, as in the case of the Middlesex Yeomanry Regiment's Museum, whose collection is now housed in the Royal Signals Museum, or into the appropriate local authority museum, like that of the Royal Devon Yeomanry, which has recently moved from a local TA centre into the Museum of North Devon.

Such amalgamations of regular and volunteer collections have taken place with notable success in a number of museums, including the Regiments of Gloucestershire Museum, and the Museum of the Duke of Edinburgh's Royal Regiment. Some believe that this kind of arrangement may provide the perfect solution to the problem of how to preserve both regular army and volunteer force museums in the face of dwindling resources, and Colonel Pip Newton (1987a:69), the ex-Secretary of AMOT, has long advocated the formation of a single military museum for each county, by amalgamating all local military collections, as a solution to this problem. A few such County Military Museums have now been formed, notably in Shropshire, Cumbria, Somerset, Lancashire and Dorset, either run by the local authority or by a joint initiative between the trustees of the collections and the MoD or local authority. This solution was praised in the MGC Report (MGC 1990:25), because not only does it preserve the volunteer force collections, but it also offers 'scope for a much more coherent account of army history in a county than can be accomplished with any one collection'. But others (see Wood 1986a and 1987a), as was noted in Chapter 3, implicitly argue against such amalgamations within local authority museums by claiming that, in some cases, military collections are not appreciated or understood by local authority curators and their political masters.

On the whole, perhaps not surprisingly for units which saw no overseas service before the Boer War, and who were rarely called upon to fire their weapons in anger, these volunteer regiments' displays tend to be dominated by examples of their colourful dress uniforms, together with pieces of mess silver, china and glass and their sporting trophies. This seems to place the emphasis on the social rather than the military side of their service – a picture reinforced by the photographs of summer camps and public parades, the ladies' regimental brooches, and the dance cards which line the walls and decorate the display cases of the Warwickshire Yeomanry Museum and of other volunteer regiments' museums. Yet this in itself may be a valuable addition to the social history of the region, as such objects and displays show how some of the local families spent their time when not carrying on their normal business. It also demonstrates another source of linkages between local individuals and families that were not dependent on work, locality or church, and which could be of value to local historians.

There was, however, a darker side to their activities which is now being acknowledged in the Museum of the Manchesters and in other museums. As has already been mentioned, in the absence of a full-time police force, the military, both regular and volunteer, had to provide the executive arm of the state to contain smuggling and to suppress riots and other civil disturbances. With the small standing army badly stretched in the early nineteenth century defending the empire, the volunteer units, and in particular the yeomanry regiments, were called upon to fill the gap. They took part, therefore, in the suppression of what the authorities regarded as public disturbances. Perhaps the most famous of these incidents took place during a meeting of 60,000 people calling for parliamentary reform on St Peter's Field in Manchester on 16 August 1819. The meeting was apparently orderly until the magistrates instructed the troops on duty there, including the Manchester Yeomanry and the 15th Hussars, to arrest the main speaker, Henry Hunt. The crowd tried to prevent this and the troops' subsequent intervention left 11 civilians dead and approximately 500 wounded. The affair became known as the Peterloo Massacre. This seminal incident helped fuel the intense hatred and suspicion of the army felt by many ordinary people during the 50 years after the Napoleonic War.

The Peterloo massacre is usually blamed on the inexperience and inadequate training of the Manchester Yeomanry, who were said to have panicked when surrounded by the mob and had to be rescued by the regular troops. Yet in the trials that followed their officers were acquitted. The Lancashire County and Regimental Museum deals with this incident in some detail and displays a sword that, the caption explains, was presented to Major Hugh Hornby Birley of the Manchester and Salford Yeomanry by his men 'to commemorate their honourable acquittal by a Grand Jury at Lancaster Assizes for the part that they had taken when called out in aid of the Civil Powers in St Peter's Field on 16 August 1819'.

Most military museums with yeomanry collections tackle to some degree the use of troops as policemen. However, few regimental and corps museums, as we have seen, examine the relationship between the military and the civilian population in much detail. One notable exception is the Museum of the Manchesters in Ashton-under-Lyne.

In 1958 the Manchester Regiment amalgamated with the King's Regiment (Liverpool), and in 1965 the regimental museum trustees transferred its collection on loan to the local authority. Twenty years later it became necessary to rehouse the collection when its previous home in Manchester's Queen's Park was converted into a workshop and conservation studio. The opportunity was taken at that time to plan a new style of military museum which would incorporate the military collection within a broader social history of the local area. The regimental artifacts displayed are fairly typical of those to be found in regimental museums, with examples of military uniforms, weapons and equipment, as well as a few souvenirs, all displayed in quite a conventional way. The history of the Manchester Regiment, and that of the local volunteer regiment, is told chronologically from the time of the formation of the Manchester Regiment's component units in the eighteenth century until its final amalgamation in 1958. But what makes this military museum so different is the emphasis placed on the interrelationship between these regiments and the town of Ashton-under-Lyne (see Preece 1987:72).

What the design achieves is the juxtaposition of this regimental display with a series of large illustrated captions which discuss relevant aspects of both military life and local social history. These captions describe life in the army in the eighteenth and nineteenth centuries in considerable detail, especially its poor pay and conditions and its harsh discipline. They then explain how and why local people were still induced to join the army. But I think the really distinctive captions are those which discuss the building of the first barracks at Ashton in 1843 (so that troops could be on hand to quell local working-class agitation) and the subsequent interaction of the army with the civilian population (Figure 7.1). These describe clearly the uneasy relationship between the regiment and the population of the town at a time when the army was not only the police force and an important local employer, but also a major customer for local suppliers of food and other essentials.

Figure 7.1 Illustrated caption in the Museum of the Manchesters: a discussion of the reasons for building the Manchester Barracks at Ashton-under-Lyne in 1843.

Source: Museum of the Manchesters, Tameside Museums and Gallery Service

The Museum of the Manchesters goes some way towards linking military history to the more general history of this country, but there are still a large number of issues concerning the interrelationship between the armed forces and the civilian population, some of which I have touched on earlier in the chapter, which cry out for more attention. The national military museums might appear the most obvious forum for this kind of exhibition or display, but perhaps Dennis Oomen (1992:49) is correct to say that this should more appropriately be handled by social history museums. In that case, it may be that we shall have to wait until a national museum of social history is set up before we can view displays which examine the true relationship between the armed forces and those they were meant to protect.

Material about the way in which servicemen interacted with the civilian population can be found, however, along with a veritable goldmine of other social history evidence, in the archives of most military museums. These treasure troves, and the uses to which they are put by military museums to inform and educate the public, will be examined in the next chapter.

Notes

1. A Guide to the Royal Engineers Museum, 1993, p.1.

8. *Military Museum Archives: Research and Education*

Illiterate letters from privates at the front giving an insight into their experiences, in fifty years' time may be rated as more interesting than official despatches.
C. Reginald Grundy (Kavanagh, G. 1984:66)

As we have seen, military museums, and in particular regimental and corps museums, have not been good at recording the social history of the ordinary soldier or sailor and his impact on those around him in their displays. Too often they have concentrated on the battles and on the pomp of military life while virtually ignoring the day-to-day existence of the servicemen and their families. We have seen how some museums are now trying to rectify this situation, while others carry on much as before. Yet, in fact, behind the scenes virtually all military museums do record in some detail the social history of the serviceman in the documents, books and other material held in their archives.

From their earliest days, military museums, including regimental museums, have seen the importance of collecting the private papers of their soldiers or sailors as well as the official documents relating to the history of their units. In 1917, for example, Sir Martin Conway, the first Director of the Imperial War Museum, said that the IWM would need to collect personal documents, publications and photographs to help vitalize the large mass of official exhibits it would be receiving (quoted in Kavanagh 1994:130). A decade later, G.M. Bland, while setting up the King's Own Royal Regiment Museum, appealed for photographs, diaries, autograph letters, portraits, maps and records in book form as well as the more usual artifacts (*Museums Journal* 1929 28,12:399), and the Black Watch Regiment seems to have originally decided to set up its museum just to house such documentary material[1]. These were not, of course, isolated cases, and the inventories of most of the early regimental museums list documents, photographs, paintings and books as part of their holdings (Cowper 1935:45).

Moreover, such papers have been amongst the most common souvenirs kept by the ordinary serviceman, and so they represent a rich source, though, it must be admitted, a rather patchy one. It is one area in which military museums are sometimes better endowed than their civilian cousins. The independent existence of county archives has meant that, often, relevant documentary material is kept in a separate building from the historical artifacts. This in turn means that the local museum will hold documentary material concerning the origins of its objects, but may have very little on the way in which they were used, or on the impact they had on people's lives. Indeed there is still a debate about whether or not social history museums should collect documents at all (Frostick 1993:210,222). A researcher interested, therefore, in the history of the use of the museum artifacts he or she wishes to study may have to make a separate visit to a different repository. Some military collections are divided in this way. The Queen's Own Highlanders, for example, have an archive and library which is under the control of their RHQ and separate from their museum, while the Royal Army Educational Corps has donated its archive to the National Army Museum to allow more space for exhibits at its museum in Beaconsfield. But in most cases paper records and objects are kept under the same roof and administered by the same staff, making access to the historical significance of the artifacts much easier for the researcher.

This arrangement can, of course, be a mixed blessing. As Colonel Peter Walton, Secretary of AMOT, reported, in a talk to the 1994 Annual Conference of the British Records Association, some military museums look after their archives well, while others do so badly, and all are loath to give up their collections to the local Record Offices. This may mean that in many cases these documentary collections are not receiving the level of professional care that historic records need and deserve. Few military museums, apart from the nationals and the larger corps museums, can afford the luxury of hiring trained archivists or librarians, or the money to spend on proper archival storage facilities. The records could then be considered at risk, though both AMOT and the National Army Museum are providing advice and assistance where they can, and in most cases the archives are in fact looked after as well as the other artifacts held by these museums. Arguably, a greater drawback to leaving these records with the regiments and corps may be the poor facilities for researchers that most of their museums can offer, which, combined with a lack of printed catalogues of their collections, make these documents less accessible to the public than they would be in a local Record Office.

The decision to retain these records is an understandable, if occasionally unfortunate one. Regimental and corps museums are, after all, considered to be the natural repository for their units' history and heritage, and, as we shall see, they are expected to be able to answer detailed questions on these topics, for which rapid access to this archival material is often essential.

Moreover, these museums are usually closely linked to their relevant RHQs, which in turn receive a number of welfare enquiries each year which can only be dealt with by reference to historic personnel or unit records. Such welfare matters constitute an important part of the work of the RHQs, and it is not surprising that they wish to have the relevant documents under regimental control rather than their being deposited in a local Record Office. It could be argued, of course, that this only applies to the more modern records, and that the truly historic archives should be handed over to professionals to conserve and protect. But it is easy to see why military museum trustees look on these records in the same light in which they view historic artifacts, and are as reluctant to give them up as they would be any other part of their collection.

The retention of some types of archival material may, however, need official sanction. All official papers relating to the armed forces are public records, and as such should be deposited in the Public Record Office. But some institutions, including, for example, the REME Museum and the Royal Military Academy Sandhurst Collection, have been inspected by officials from the Public Record Office and granted the status of Authorised Places of Deposit. They are thus effectively Public Record Office outstations and can hold official records[2]. They have, of course, to abide by the restrictions imposed by the Official Secrets Act and by the provisions of the Public Records Acts of 1958 and 1967. Therefore, some personnel records that they might hold will be closed to anyone but the next of kin for 75 years, and documents relating to crimes and punishment to everyone for 75 years after the date of the last entry in the relevant register. But this means that all the papers from the period covered by this study should be available for research.

The MoD is anxious to protect all the various documents held in its military museums and insists that, in order to ensure their preservation, records which are not required for use or display should be placed in the care of the National Army Museum or the local authority Record Office. But as we have noted, most museums can find reasons for keeping the documents entrusted to them, and rarely hand them over to another repository unless they can no longer cope with them or are forced to close. The archive of the Middlesex Regiment, for example, was given to the National Army Museum when its museum closed, while the Royal Sussex Regiment's archive was passed to the West Sussex Record Office when its other historic collections were placed in the Sussex Combined Services Museum.

The kinds of records to be found in military museums are varied but normally comprise regimental records, such as muster rolls, mess accounts, copies of daily orders and, for the modern period, copies of unit war diaries and histories; examples of individual records such as pay books, attestation forms, records of service and discharge papers; private papers like letters and diaries, memoirs and biographies; official printed documents and books, including maps, reports, and campaign histories; and a mass of illustrative material such as prints, drawings and photographs. Twentieth-century events may also be documented by film and sound records.

The value of these sources varies, of course, from type to type and even from example to example. Dr Peter Boyden, head of the Archives section of the National Army Museum, has remarked (Boyden 1987:36) that regimental records, for instance, are of considerable importance to genealogists and others seeking to reconstruct the lives of past generations of soldiers, but goes on to remind researchers that 'it has never been a function of the British Government to create records and collect data for the benefit of future generations of historians'. The official material which survives, therefore, will have been prepared to provide the information the government needed in the way it needed it, and may have to be carefully analyzed and interpreted to yield the kind of data the historian or genealogist wants.

Moreover, Boyden explains that, while there were regulations specifying which records were to be kept and where, these regulations were not always adhered to, so that data which should have survived has been lost, and documents which should have been destroyed have survived, often in private hands or museum archives. Thus the Public Record Office has some of the many annual returns (including muster books, pay lists and casualty returns) which commanding officers of regular units had to submit to army headquarters, but those for the militia and the volunteer units have been destroyed (Boyden 1987:44). At the same time the regimental books, which were held by the regiments, and in which information about supplies, food and individual service records were kept, are badly scattered and very unevenly preserved. Personal records are, of course, even more vulnerable to the ravages of time, and comparatively few collections from the years covered by this book are held in museum archives, though the number increases dramatically for the twentieth century.

Nevertheless many important and useful documents do survive, and, while it would be tedious in the extreme to consider every type of document that the researcher might come across in military archives, a few examples will help to illustrate the depth and breadth of useful information that can be locked up in such sources.

Muster rolls, for example, in which are recorded the names of men serving in a particular regiment at a given time, are rather dry documents. Yet they may contain a wealth of useful information. For the military historian they can show the actual, as opposed to the nominal, strength of a unit at a precise time, as well as giving the names of its officers, which might help to verify the military service of a famous military figure. The local historian may gain a good insight into the geographic spread of the unit's recruits by comparing the soldiers' names with those surnames native to certain areas, while the family historian can see if an ancestor was serving in the regiment at that time. The Warwickshire Yeomanry Museum has just such a document on display – a troop roll of 1831, which shows the names of local men who joined up as volunteers at that time.

Messing records and unit account books can shed considerable light on the diet of soldiers and their officers, on the cost of such provisions and on their sources. Casualty returns, on the other hand, can tell us about the health of servicemen at a particular time, showing which diseases they were prone to and what proportion of them actually became battle casualties. A good example is the discharge book in the Royal Marines Museum which details the injuries, infirmities and diseases suffered by Marines that caused them to be unfit for further service.

Where they exist and are available for research, pension records may contain a wealth of information about the service records of both officers and men in the pension applications submitted by their widows, as well as showing what proportion of the servicemen lived to draw their own pension. Some knowledge can even be gleaned indirectly from the men's attestation papers and the description books kept by the regiments about both the state of health of the civilian population and of the general economic conditions. These records, which were completed for each recruit and constituted the first part of his military service history, contain some useful details, including age and height on enlistment, place of birth and civilian trade. This information, from which can be calculated the average height of this sample of the population, combined with any surviving records concerning how many men were rejected after their medicals and why (and this information is generally available from the period of the Boer War onwards), can give an indication of the nation's health at the time. Moreover, as men frequently joined the army because there was no work for them anywhere else, these attestation records can also show which trades were doing badly at any particular time or in any specific location.

Unit orders, on the other hand, provide a more basic insight into the life and work of the unit. They record the names of men joining or leaving, and of those receiving punishment or being promoted. They also give details of any unit movements and list individuals' duties. They thus provide a rich tapestry of information, though this has to be sifted to find the pearls amongst the routine dross. Their counterpart, the unit war diary, may furnish a valuable record of the unit's experiences within a particular military campaign. These documents record the movements and activities of both the unit as a whole and its individual members, and often list casualties or medal winners. They are an excellent source, though they usually date only from the beginning of this century. Moreover, they were frequently the responsibility of the most junior officer and were not always as contemporary and well informed as they might appear. They are nevertheless useful documents for both the military and family historian as they show who did what, and when.

For the modern period, there are other published and unpublished records which are important source material for military historians. The official campaign records, for example, can give a historian a good understanding of the way in which particular actions were fought, and how each specific battle fitted into the overall campaign, something which is not always clear, it must be admitted, from the displays in military museums. Moreover, the military training handbooks and manuals of the period can provide useful insights into the training methods and the strategies and tactics in use at the time, and into the limitations imposed on these by contemporary weapons. Indeed, in the modern section of the archives of military museums can often be found user handbooks and manuals on guns, missiles, tanks, ships, aeroplanes and small arms, together with those for other vital equipment such as radios, vehicles and computers. These can provide the raw material to enable future historians to understand the nature of warfare in the second half of the twentieth century.

Other records can provide useful information for the social historian. Since the First World War regiments and corps have formed old comrades' associations which organize reunions, act as a conduit for men and women to maintain contact with their comrades and provide, when necessary, access to funds to help those who have fallen on hard times. They often produce a magazine, and that, combined with their unpublished records, provides an invaluable insight into life after military service.

By far the richest jewels to be found in the archives of these military museums, though, are holdings of private papers. These papers comprise the documents that soldiers and sailors have retained from their period of military service and which eventually they or their families have passed to the museum. In the main, such collections contain copies of attestation, pay, service and discharge papers, which may not seem exciting, but, as has been noted, they give details about the civilian trade and physical condition of the serviceman, together with a list of the places in which he served and the reasons for his eventual discharge. They will also contain information about pay and promotions, and can therefore provide much valuable material about the individual for the genealogist or social historian.

Occasionally these collections also contain the serviceman's letters and diaries, which may constitute a very important historical source. Clearly, before the nineteenth century, literate soldiers or sailors were a rarity. Even officers were not always able to read and write. Diaries or correspondence from this period are therefore not common, and this is particularly true of the periods between 1660 and 1680 and between 1713 and 1756, for some unknown reason (McGuffie 1964:xxii).

But those which exist often give exciting and useful insights into a serviceman's life from enlistment to discharge. Moreover, such documents grow in number as literacy within the armed forces increased, so that by the beginning of this century it was quite common for servicemen of all ranks to keep diaries or to write letters home; military museum archives are fortunate to hold many examples of these.

It also became more common for servicemen to write their memoirs, and these also appear in military museum libraries or archives. Like any examples of personal accounts, not all of these records are totally innocent and they have to be treated with caution. As one compiler of an anthology of military memoirs has noted, 'one or two are laconic, others are loquacious . . . none of them, it must be remembered, is on oath . . . (and) some were undoubtedly written for effect'. He also adds a caveat about the strengths and weaknesses of the picture painted by these records. He points out that 'some sides of military service tend to be very fully treated, others are somewhat empty; there is naturally more about victories than about defeats, less on the practical details of weaponry . . . than on discipline'. Nevertheless he concludes that 'in one way or another, a great deal of truth about the life of an ordinary soldier in peace and war becomes apparent from (their) pages' (McGuffie 1964:xxiii).

The compiler of a similar anthology, based on servicemen's letters written between 1450 and 1900, draws his reader's attention to the common feelings and beliefs amongst these men, despite the vast differences in time in which they were writing (Sanger 1993). But he also claims that these letters provide not only the most vivid description of battles, but express the experience of warfare more immediately and truthfully than any retrospective history could.

Even allowing for the natural bias of their authors, these letters, diaries and personal accounts are clearly a rich source for the social history of military service. Increasingly, military museums are making use of these documentary sources both to help them with the preparation of the captions for exhibitions and as display objects in their own right. They feature, for example, in the displays of the Museum of the Duke of Edinburgh's Royal Regiment and in those of the Regiments of Gloucestershire Museum.

They are not ideal display items because they have particular conservation problems, and it is rarely easy for the public to read the significant passages because of the handwriting or because entries are spread over several pages. But more and more museums, including the new military gallery which Ian Whitehead has developed for Tyne and Wear Museums Service, are finding ways of overcoming these practical problems, because such archival material enables museums to represent aspects of the individual soldier's experiences which are not easy to show using artifacts or conventional paintings (Taylor 1993:4).

Even if the original manuscripts cannot be used on display, extracts from them can make interesting and informative additions to display captions. The Museum of the 14th/20th King's Hussars in the Lancashire County and Regimental Museum makes such a use of the 'several accounts written by the 19th century soldiers recording their lives at home and abroad' which it holds in its archive. Extracts from personal diaries, letters and other documents link individuals to particular events in the Museum of the King's Regiment (Liverpool) displays, and they also form the basis of a description, under the title 'The Soldiers' Tale', of the Battle of Qatia in 1916, in the Regiments of Gloucestershire Museum.

But even single documents can help to add a personal dimension to a description of a campaign. The Guards' Museum uses a letter describing the death of Ensign Buckridge to illustrate the Battle of Burgos with a poignancy that no official account could achieve. The Museum of the King's Regiment (Liverpool) draws on a selection of documents, including the manuscript diary of Thomas Evans describing the Battle of Alexandria, Private John Whitworth's papers from his peacetime service in India between 1871 and 1879 and the siege of Ladysmith diary of Captain C.J. Steavenson, to cover aspects of military life and history which would not be easy to recount using artifacts alone.

Greater use could be made of such manuscript material by military museums, though there is the real danger to be avoided of simply turning these museum displays into books on the wall. Utilized sparingly this documentary material can add great depth to a display, as the Museum of the King's Regiment (Liverpool) and the Lancashire County and Regimental Museum have shown.

Paintings, prints and drawings are also a mainstay of many military museum displays and research collections. They can, as has been discussed in Chapter 4, portray battles, sieges and skirmishes, often based on eyewitness accounts or drawn by a talented participant. For all their weaknesses, they may be the only available visual record of such events. They can also, perhaps more successfully, illustrate uniforms and equipment from periods when original examples no longer exist. The Guards Museum has a splendid collection of prints of the uniforms of its various units at different times, and most museums have similar examples. Illustrations of this type are, moreover, often the sole visual record we have of servicemen carrying out their daily tasks in this period. Drawings and prints may also be the only way in which soldiers' or sailors' humour can be shown; the Royal Marines Museum, for instance, has a fine set of cartoons on display. Many other examples of visual material lie in the personal diaries and letters held in military museum archives.

Photographs are another common source for the period after the middle of the nineteenth century, and are routinely collected by military museums without the reservations which seem to trouble some social history curators (Green 1993:202). As we have seen, photographs of battles were quite rare until the twentieth century because the speed of the film used before that time was too slow to allow for action shots. Early photography was good, however, at portraiture, and any number of nineteenth-century photographs remain, showing individuals or groups in military uniforms; all too often, though, they lack the captions which would make them truly invaluable sources.

Photographs can also give an insight into aspects of military life not normally covered in much detail in other sources. By the last quarter of the nineteenth century photography had become quite a popular hobby, and many military collections contain private photograph albums from the 1880s and 1890s showing units in camp, on parade or going about their daily business. The Warwickshire Yeomanry Museum, for example, has a fine collection of private photograph albums showing its soldiers at work and at play at their summer camps in the late Victorian and Edwardian periods. The Royal Signals Museum has similar albums which show, amongst other things, how particular pieces of equipment were actually used. In examples like these, a picture can indeed be worth a thousand words.

Photographs are also very useful display items. They are easier to copy successfully than documents and so avoid the conservation problems inherent in displaying original papers. Being visual, the visitor can take in their meaning more immediately. They can be used to illustrate particular points or to bring to life themes, like camp life, ceremonial duties or sport, which are not successfully illustrated by artifacts alone. They need to be treated with some caution, of course, because, before the advent of fast film in the twentieth century, most photographs of people had to be posed, and in any case photographs are still selective images. But they can show the large scene or the small detail, and are an invaluable source for the military and social historian, the curator and the museum visitor.

Cine-film is also a major source for the twentieth century, and has been used to cover most of the major and many of the minor military conflicts involving British troops since the outbreak of the First World War. Movie cameras, and latterly television cameras, have also been turned on the armed forces going about their daily lives and duties; film and video will be invaluable research tools in the future. Military museums already use film to illustrate their twentieth century history, and often have a film archive which can be made available to researchers, though the period they show falls outside that of this study.

Oral history is another archival source growing in scale and importance. Most of the national military museums have departments or programmes dedicated to the recording of the experiences of servicemen and women, and most regimental and corps museums have some taped interviews. Like most other sources, oral history has to be approached with caution. Memories fade and become distorted by what has been learnt since the event being recalled, and people are likely to suppress subconsciously memories which show them in a bad light. On the other hand they may well remember details, or even feelings, which they have never recorded before in any other form, which makes this a worthwhile source. Oral history recordings can also provide a useful adjunct to exhibitions as a commentary accompanying a display or tableau describing how a particular piece of equipment was used or performed, or by relating some personal experience of the event being portrayed. Obviously, oral history recordings are not available for the period covered by this book.

As well as this archival material, military museums usually have libraries containing published unit histories, autobiographies, biographies and reference books on subjects like uniforms, weapons, equipment and vehicles. Military history is still a very popular area for publications, and many new books and magazine articles are published each year. Military curators are able, therefore, for a fairly modest outlay, to build up a sizable specialist reference library. As J.R. Kenyon (1992:586) has said, such a library 'forms an essential core of any academic institution ... (and) ... it is one of the most important educational resources a museum can possess'. Without it, he argues, the curator is unable to fulfil his or her duties to the museum or to the public.

These military museum archives and libraries can act as a valuable resource for curators researching the story-lines for exhibitions or the details for captions. Some even use them to provide the raw material for their own research projects. Lieutenant-Colonel (Retd) George Forty, ex-Director and Curator of the Tank Museum, is a prolific author of books and articles on tanks and other military subjects, and one or two other military museum curators have established reputations as military historians. But as many curators are only part-time in the first place, or, like the majority of their civilian colleagues, have little time to carry out their own research, this is not a major use for these resources.

Increasingly, however, these archives are a source of information being tapped by the general public. The MGC Working Party noted (MGC 1990:28) that a large proportion of the average military museum curator's time is spent in dealing with written enquiries which will involve researching the regimental library and archives. The number of these enquiries is increasing, it observed, and they come not only from those with a specific interest in military history, but also from people conducting family history research[3]. Some museums receive more than 1000 such enquiries a year and, the Report claimed, this 'service is an aspect of museum activity as important as providing visual interpretation through displays. For regimental and corps museums it is often a major element of the service provided to the public ... though one which goes largely unrecognised, most importantly, by the MoD whose only performance indicators are visitor numbers and earned income' (MGC 1990:28).

Another growing call on the curator's time is providing an educational service. Originally, as we saw in Chapter 2, military museums were usually set up in regimental depots, and their formation was justified partly in terms of the training facility they provided for recruits. With the centralization of recruit training, this function decreased in importance, and as the MGC Report noted, regimental museums are no longer 'regarded as an essential concomitant to training programmes' (MGC 1990:23), and indeed it is now very rare to find an army training regiment sharing a barracks with a military museum[4]. Corps museums, on the other hand, which are mostly sited in training centres, 'are usually regarded as having a clear training and education role for the serving soldier' (MGC 1990:23), and their curators play a considerable part in the use of their museums for teaching aspects of corps history, or the history of the technical subject they display, to serving members of their corps.

In addition, however, military museum curators have always provided guided tours of their museums for both official visitors, the general public and school parties. Now such tours are no longer enough. Increasingly, curators are called upon to give talks on their collections away from their museums to clubs, local historical societies and other bodies. But the biggest increase in demand has been from schools. The National Curriculum places great emphasis on the use of original material in the teaching of all subjects, and teachers are turning to military museums to loan items and provide talks and handling sessions on a variety of historical and technical subjects.

Regimental museums rarely have the luxury of a separate education officer, though the national museums now have such specialists. The National Army Museum's Education Department, for example, 'caters for all age groups, from primary to sixth-form, colleges and beyond'[5]. It claims that it helps pupils and teachers make the best and most enjoyable use of the Museum's resources, through the handling of objects and the study of contemporary documents and illustrations, to create links with the past. Visits to the Education Department usually begin with a session of one and a half hours which makes use of slides, music and object handling, allowing students to try on Civil War armour, handle a musket or smell a tin of chocolate sent by Queen Victoria to troops during the Boer War. These sessions always pay attention 'to the social aspects of the Army, as well as relating military events to a wider historical perspective'. In addition to these sessions the Education Department provides a range of facsimile military documents, reading lists and activity sheets, runs study days, model-making classes and holiday events and gives advice on class and individual projects. As we have seen, it also organizes re-enactment events in the museum to bring various aspects of military history to life, and provides an input into the planning of displays to ensure that they have an educational dimension (Talbot Rice 1984:14). The size and diversity of its collection means that, in addition to military and social history, it can offer educational material on needlework, art and technology and a variety of other topics.

The Gurkha Museum also finds ways of using its collections to help schools teach aspects of the National Curriculum other than military history. It offers material on food and farming and land transport by drawing on Nepalese artifacts. It provides an outreach service to schools and a loan collection, as well as museum-based programmes (Richards 1991:24). Indeed most military museums can offer a wide range of learning experiences because, as Christine Beresford has noted, 'their collections embrace a number of disciplines including the fine and decorative arts, technology, ethnography and social history' (1991:27).

Most military museums cannot match the level of provision available to the national museums with the staff and resources they are allowed, though most try to provide some sort of educational service. They can, however, often call on the help and advice of external education specialists in drawing up their educational programmes. In Dorset, for example, small local museums, including the military museums, can obtain advice and some practical assistance from two local authority education officers, and military museums belonging to the Hampshire-based Defence of the Realm consortium could call on the services of an educational coordinator provided for this purpose by Hampshire County Council. The local Area Museums Councils will also give advice on educational matters, as will AMOT.

Many military museums are also part of the local authority museum provision, and can, therefore, enjoy the benefits of being connected with the local educational service. On its formation the Durham Light Infantry Museum and Arts Centre, for example, came under the county's Education Department. There was a special emphasis placed on the use of the museum by schools, and the museum was therefore given expert guidance in the preparation of its teachers' notes, worksheets, questionnaires and gallery talks (*Museums Journal* 1975 75,3:13).

In whatever way the education service is provided, military curators are having to look at their collections in new ways to enable them to see their true potential as teaching aids. Major John Ellis, Curator of the Cheshire Military Museum, has, for example, persuaded his local college to use documents held in his museum's archive as primary source material for two modules of a Victorian Studies Master's degree and hopes to develop his contacts with Higher Education teachers in future years. In general, though, military museum curators need to communicate more effectively with the staff of the science and history departments of schools, universities and colleges to make them more aware of what their museums have to offer. Progress is being made, however, and, as Colonel Peter Walton of AMOT has argued[6], this is a vital field of future development for regimental and corps museums.

Another aspect of this educational work, and one in which extensive use can be made of archival material, is the preparation of museum guides. These guides are sometimes just what the name suggests, a plan of the exhibition showing the route to take, and giving a brief history of the unit and of the major objects to be seen in each section of the display. Particularly good examples of this kind of guide are available in the Royal Green Jackets Museum and in the Border Regiment Museum.

Other booklets, though loosely described as museum guides, are in fact less concerned with providing a plan of the museum than with filling in some of the historical detail which cannot be crammed into the display captions. The National Army Museum, for instance, produces small books to accompany exhibitions like 'The Road To Waterloo', which incorporate the fruits of the research for the exhibition, and which can cover a 'wide variety of subjects from equipment . . . to disease among the soldiers . . . ' (Robertson 1991:26). Not only do these books extend the scope of the exhibition, but they act as important academic studies in their own right. For many years the National Army Museum also published an Annual Report which allowed it to describe to a wider audience different aspects of its collections or to mention new acquisitions. This acted as an on-going catalogue to the collection and as a showplace for small pieces of research carried out by its staff.

Less ambitious booklets, drawing on, but not slavishly following, the displays and museum objects, and intended, in part at least, as souvenirs of the visit (Bassett 1993:616), can be found in a number of military museum shops, and they provide a similar broad history of their subject. The Scottish United Services Museum's booklet, *Story of the Scottish Soldier 1660–1914* by Jenni Calder, the Royal Marines Museum's *The Story of Britain's Sea Soldiers* by Matthew Little and the Royal Naval Museum's guide *The Royal Navy in Peace and War* by Colin White are good examples of this kind of potted history.

This type of booklet, like the excellent children's guide produced by the Regimental Museum of the Queen's Own Hussars, allows the curators to set their collections more firmly within a social or military history context than is usually achieved in the displays of artifacts or through exhibition captions. It is often in these booklets, in fact, that a number of the topics concerning the life of the servicemen, such as recruiting, billeting, pay, promotion, discipline, health, food and family life, which seem to receive scant attention in the displays, are examined in considerable detail. Perhaps this is in part because curators find it easier to deal with these topics via the written word than through exhibitions, or possibly they believe that the main concern of their displays should be the telling of the story of the military achievements of their unit or service, rather than dealing with these more general matters. But in any case, these booklets provide a valuable part of the educational provision on offer in these museums, and are often their main vehicle for telling the social history of their soldiers or sailors.

This concentration in their public displays on the history and glorious achievements of their particular unit, which can lead to a rather narrow and parochial focus is probably unavoidable in these regimental and corps museums, but should not apply, perhaps, to the national military museums with their broader terms of reference. These museums will be examined in the next chapter.

Notes

1. Letter from Major (Retd) A.R. McKinnell, MBE, Curator of the Black Watch Museum to the author, 1 November 1994, drawing on an extract from the regimental journal, *The Red Hackle*, January 1925.
2. Letter from Colonel Peter Walton to the author, 7 February 1995.
3. The Essex Regiment Museum maintains a card index of Essex County servicemen to help answer family history enquiries.
4. Letter from Colonel Walton *op. cit.*
5. National Army Museum leaflet *Educational Services*, n.d.
6. Letter from Colonel Walton *op. cit.*

9. *The National Perspective*

National Museums ought to act as the reflectors of the history of that nation's political decisions.

(S. Wood 1987b:66)

Throughout this book I have been looking at the way in which various aspects of our military history have been shown in the 150 or so museums with military collections. What seems to have emerged is that, while some of these museums try to look at broader issues or set their story within a wider context, most fall short of providing a general military, social or political history of the armed forces of the period because they are primarily concerned with telling the story of their own particular regiment, corps, service or locality. Taken together they have, I think, a full and interesting story to tell, but singly they are often disappointing in their coverage of more general military or social history.

It could be argued, therefore, that there is a place for a national perspective drawing together the various threads and setting our military history within a social and political history framework. There are indeed four national museums dedicated to some aspects of the military history of Britain in the period I am reviewing: the Royal Armouries, the Scottish United Services Museum, the National Army Museum and the National Maritime Museum. The Imperial War Museum begins its coverage with the First World War, as does the RAF Museum, and so they fall outside the chronological scope of this book. I have referred to aspects of the collections of each of these relevant national museums at other places in this study, but they are important museums and will now be considered separately in more detail.

The Royal Armouries

The oldest of them by far are the Royal Armouries in the Tower of London. They owe their origins to the use of the Tower as a depot for the military weapons and equipment of the Royal Forces from the thirteenth century onwards (MGC 1990:10). Later the Tower became the headquarters of the Board of Ordnance and was a major arsenal for military and naval weapons. By the process of 'accidental accumulation' that I described in Chapter 1, the Royal Armouries became the repository of a substantial collection of arms and armour, which has acted as the basis for a museum since the 1680s.

The collection now contains arms and armour of historical, technical and artistic interest from Britain, Europe and the Near, Middle and Far East. The Trustees of the Royal Armouries have also recently established an outstation at Fort Nelson near Portsmouth, where they can display some of their collection of artillery pieces.

The location of the museum of the Royal Armouries within the Tower has meant that it has regularly enjoyed over two million visitors a year, making it easily the most popular military collection in the country. But lack of space has ensured that only a proportion of its collection can be displayed. The Trustees of the Royal Armouries are now having a purpose-built museum constructed in Leeds where they hope to show off those parts of the collection which are not specific to the Tower of London. This will enable the museum to 'tell the story of arms and armour around the world up to the present' (Wilson 1993:33), and to offer better educational and visitor facilities.

Clearly, this is a very specialized collection which contains few of the everyday artifacts or historic souvenirs which allow other military museums to deal with a variety of military and social history topics. The Royal Armouries' education officers have developed techniques to set the collections within their social context and to use them to discuss issues like the role of women in military history (Wilkinson and Hughes 1991:24). But the Royal Armouries tell the story of the development of arms and armour, not the history of the armed forces, and one has to turn to the other national military museums to gain a more detailed view of the military and social history of these forces.

The Scottish United Services Museum

The Scottish United Services Museum in Edinburgh was founded in 1930 as the Scottish National Naval and Military Museum, when, under the direction of the Duke of Atholl, 'a building adjoining the Scottish National War Memorial was reconstructed to form a museum to house the trophies and relics of Scottish regiments' (*Museums Journal* 1930 29, 9:324). It now owes its national status to the fact that it is part of the National Museums of Scotland. Its position within Edinburgh Castle gives it a considerable advantage over many other museums because it is assured of attracting a substantial proportion of the Castle's one million visitors a year, and so does not have to justify its existence (Wood 1987b:65).

Its mandate covers all three armed services, though in 1990 it was forced to close its East Gallery, which had contained displays on the Scottish yeomanry, the Royal Scots Dragoon Guards, the Royal Navy and the Royal Air Force, as part of the overall plan for the redevelopment of Edinburgh Castle. These artifacts have had to be placed in store until new space is made available for them. Until then, the museum's displays concentrate on the Scottish soldier, because that gallery has been left intact, though the material on the other arms can be inspected in the store (Wood 1990:210).

In the 1960s the museum organized a series of annual meetings with representatives of the Scottish regimental museums, at which it was agreed that the national museum would concentrate on 'military history as an academic subject, the professional display of military specimens, and research leading to accurate recording of facts . . .' (Thorburn 1962:194), while the regimental museums would deal with everything connected with the life of the regiment,'and their need to function as a *salle d'honneur* was recognised'. An employee of the museum at that time, W. A. Thorburn, claimed (1962:194) that it was 'the first museum in Britain to show military material as related historical objects, rather than mere relics . . . '

But no matter how ahead of its time it was in the 1960s, photographs of its displays taken in the early 1980s suggest that it had come to resemble an old-fashioned regimental museum. In fact its Director, Stephen Wood, admitted in 1986 (Wood 1986a:14) that its average lay visitor became 'apparently visually concussed' upon 'being confronted with case after case packed with the arcane material culture of the Scottish serviceman'. He concluded that 'as they stand at present the bulk of the displays . . . are aimed at students of military antiquities'.

He blamed the lack of change between 1945 and 1970 on inadequate funding and staffing, and since then on 'the pariah status of military museums' amongst museum professionals which ensured 'a permanent place for the Museum at the back of most queues on the very few occasions when any money was available' (Wood 1986a:15). But in 1980 the museum acquired a new building, and in 1987 the new block was opened to the public with a display called 'The Story Of The Scottish Soldier 1600–1914', illustrating the experience of the Scottish soldier and the growth of Scottish regiments, which was aimed at making 'this sub-stratum of the social history of Scotland easily intelligible to the people who form the bulk of visitors to the castle' (Wood 1986a:15).

The story of the Scottish soldier is divided into a number of chronological chunks, beginning with the formation of the standing army and ending with the First World War. The displays seem fairly conventional, with a preponderance of uniforms, weapons and paintings, though there are also several very good tableaux showing soldiers from different periods at rest, in camp or in action. What is comparatively unusual, though, is the degree to which each artifact is linked to the story of the individual who wore or used it, thereby personalizing history to a greater extent than is common in most military museums. This personal history is emphasized even more by the frequent use of extracts in the captions from the letters and diaries of soldiers, which gives a contemporary and personal perspective on all the events shown.

The exhibition also tackles a number of broader political issues. It discusses Scottish religious divisions and how these, together with opposition in some quarters to the union with England, led to instability in the country, culminating in the two Jacobite rebellions, which in turn forced the British government to maintain a standing army in Scotland between 1660 and 1750. It also highlights the suspicions regarding the loyalty of Scottish soldiers felt by the central government until well into the nineteenth century, which had to be balanced against the need for more troops to guard the empire. This led on the one hand to an initial reluctance to raise volunteer forces in Scotland, and on the other to a great enthusiasm for sending Scottish troops abroad. The captions also make it clear that there were very good practical reasons for Scots to join the British Army, as it was often their only guaranteed way of earning a living following the Highland Clearances.

The Scottish perspective is refreshing and important, given the setting for this museum and the relative paucity of material on Scottish soldiers in sites south of the border. But, despite the exhibition's emphasis on the individual soldier and its mention of such topics as recruiting, pay and conditions, the social history of soldiering is not dealt with in any great depth. Clearly, though, all exhibitions are a compromise between space and content, and the Museum has managed to cover a number of topics in a relatively small area, without turning the gallery into a book on the wall. And, as was noted in Chapter 8, it has a guide, *The Story of the Scottish Soldier 1600–1914*, which does discuss all these subjects in more detail.

As the display captions demonstrate, its archive contains a wealth of material on the daily life of the soldier, complementing the broader picture presented by the gallery. Indeed, the museum sees itself as a major centre for research into the history of Scotland's armed forces, and it maintains a substantial library and a collection of military prints, as well as its documentary holdings and reserve collection, administered by the relevant specialist staff. Material is available for research purposes and is widely consulted.

The Scottish United Services Museum also has a pastoral role as well as its normal museum functions. It offers advice on professional, technical and historical matters to the regimental museums in Scotland. A similar role is played by the National Army Museum.

The National Army Museum

Military historians had long dreamt of the foundation of a National Army Museum. In the 1950s a few enthusiasts began to plan the creation of a museum to celebrate the long history of the regular and auxiliary forces of the British Army. They included Colonel Ogilby, who founded AMOT, and his ally, Field Marshal Sir Gerald Templer, who was later to be instrumental in turning this dream into a reality through his fundraising efforts and by the persuasive force he brought to bear on the MoD. The National Army Museum (NAM) was finally established in 1960 in the former riding school at the Royal Military Academy at Sandhurst.

Initially it had under its control the historic collections of the armies of the East India Company and of the Imperial Indian Army. These had originally been brought together at the Royal Military Academy

Sandhurst after the Partition of India, as there had been no natural home for them in Britain. The National Army Museum also inherited the cavalry collections and the Irish regiment collections which had accumulated in the Royal Military Academy Sandhurst Museum[1] for the same reason. But it soon acquired, through appeals to the regiments and corps of the British Army for historic artifacts, by direct donations and purchases and by the transfer of many of the artifacts and documents from the Royal United Service Institution Museum, a sizable collection of its own. The Sandhurst site proved inadequate for the immense amount of material the Museum now held, and an appeal was launched in June 1965, on the 150th anniversary of the Battle of Waterloo, to raise the money needed to construct a purpose-built museum in central London. The new museum was opened on its Chelsea site in 1971 and was further extended in 1980.

The original and seemingly unchanging aim of the National Army Museum, incorporated in its charter, is the preservation and presentation of the story of the British Army, so as to make the achievements of the army more widely known to the general public. It is thus the public face of the army, despite the claim of its first Director at the Chelsea site, William Reid, that it was not a museum for the British Army but about the British Army (quoted in Wood 1986b:21), and it is directly funded by the MoD. The potential danger of this situation is that this museum might take extreme care to avoid showing the army in a bad light, and one might expect, therefore, that its displays would be bland and self-congratulatory. That this is not so is a credit to the professionalism of its staff and to the independence of its trustees.

The pre-1980s museum concentrated on showing 'the development of the equipment, organisation, training and administration of the army; its professional and social activities at home and abroad; its victories and defeats; and the personalities of some of its greatest leaders' (Reid 1971:63), through fairly conventional displays of uniforms, badges, medals and weapons. It even had cases devoted to famous individuals, which were referred to at the time by a journalist as 'hero-boxes' (Reid 1971:63). Gradually, however, the style of exhibition began to change, along with the kind of message that the displays conveyed. Now the museum's permanent galleries tell a broader story. They still follow the main campaigns and show the development of army uniforms, weapons, equipment, organization and tactics, but they now also focus on the social history of the soldiers who made up this army. Indeed the Museum's five-year corporate plan, *The Way Forward*, includes the primary objective to 'stress the history of the army as part of the social history of the kingdom, and thereby appeal to a much wider cross-section of the population'. To achieve this, it claims that the new displays and related publications are intended to show that 'the story of how soldiers lived, worked and, on occasion, died, is as important as changes in the art of war' (Robertson 1991:26).

As we have seen, the NAM's displays 'The Road To Waterloo' and 'The Victorian Soldier' deal with a number of issues that are not generally encountered in regimental museums. These include such topics as the social differences between officers and men, the use of foreign mercenaries and colonial troops, the growing complexity of army organization and the place of women in military history. These displays, moreover, examine the supply and quality of the uniforms and equipment issued to the men and discuss how well these items actually functioned.

The use of three life stories in 'The Victorian Soldier' gallery's audio-visual display also means the museum can explore other issues like recruitment, discipline and the fate of ex-soldiers in a way that the material artifacts displayed on their own would not allow. The other unusual feature of its displays, the use of life-sized models in reproduction uniforms, enables the NAM to show more clearly than most military museums the reality of the soldier's experience of living and fighting in mud, the cold or heat of a foreign campaign. These are not the tailor's dummies dressed in their perfect ceremonial uniforms used in most displays, but instead are representations of real men and women in real life and death situations. Displayed with them are cooking utensils, musical instruments, letters and diaries, trade tokens, writing boxes and toiletries which 'have emerged from over 30 years in storage' (Robertson 1991:26).

Yet despite the great strides it has made in bringing the soldier into the centre of the displays, the National Army Museum still has to cater to some extent for its specialist community. Models of soldiers caked in mud stand next to cases with examples of gorgets or belt buckles displayed like a taxonomic series. Perhaps this is unavoidable, for a large percentage of the particular community that regularly visits military museums expects to be able to see such technical displays; the army's national museum can hardly fail to cater for them. But it is a difficult path for the NAM to tread, and at the moment it seems to be seeking, like its logo, 'to retain allusions to the Museum's historical content and official status, but with a fresher and more contemporary approach'[2].

Like the Scottish United Services Museum, the work of the National Army Museum is not restricted to its public displays. Its educational work was alluded to in Chapter 8, and it has a large archive of books, photographs, pictures, documents and audio-visual material (which is particularly strong for the Crimean and Boer Wars), as well as a substantial reserve collection which can be consulted by researchers. Its specialist staff administer these reserve collections and provide training, expert advice and assistance to other army museums as part of the Museum's official role (MGC 1990:21). It has also influenced the way these museums have evolved. The redesign of the Regiments of Gloucestershire Museum, for example, with its innovative new emphasis on the social history of soldiering, was achieved with the help of the National Army Museum (Beresford 1991:27).

The Royal Navy does not have, as yet, an equivalent of the National Army Museum, though one national museum, the National Maritime Museum, and one designated museum, the Royal Naval Museum, have substantial naval collections.

The National Maritime Museum

The National Maritime Museum, Greenwich, was founded in 1934 by the Society for Nautical Research, with money largely provided by one of its members, Sir James Caird, a Scottish shipowner, who was also one of the main private backers for the preservation of HMS *Victory*. It is housed in the buildings of the Royal Hospital School, which date from 1807 to 1876, though it also incorporates the Queen's House and the Royal Observatory buildings. Its collections began with paintings which were previously held in the Painted Hall of the Royal Naval College and artifacts from that college's Naval Museum. It is covered in this survey because it deals with all aspects of the story of this country's involvement with the sea, which includes, of course, the Royal Navy. As the MGC Report stated, 'among the many themes it pursues is the growth of the permanent navy, and the ways in which technical and navigational innovations have influenced, or been influenced by, the history of sea defence' (MGC 1990:10). But it is not a museum of the Royal Navy as such, and so cannot be compared exactly with the other military museums examined here.

The museum tells the story of Britain and the sea from prehistoric times to the present day. Displays relevant to this study are divided into a number of galleries, some depicting aspects of ship construction or handling, and others recounting the history of Britain's sea power. In 'The Ships Of War 1650–1815' gallery, for example, some of the museum's ship model collection is used to illustrate the way naval ship design developed in that period, while in the small 'The Way Of A Ship' gallery, films and artifacts are used to demonstrate a number of aspects of ship handling, including communications at sea, navigation, ballasting and the use of anchors. Other small galleries examine how wooden naval ships were constructed, what caused them to deteriorate and how they were repaired.

The history of British sea power is dealt with in a series of displays, beginning with one which examines the foundation of the Royal Navy. This early period is illustrated with items from the *Mary Rose*, and the defeat of the Spanish Armada is explained in some detail. Later sections deal with the Anglo-Dutch Wars of the seventeenth century and the subsequent formation of a permanent, professional Royal Navy.

The strongest part of this historical sequence, however, consists of the material relating to the French Revolutionary and Napoleonic Wars. At the heart of this collection lie the Nelson memorabilia. These include trophies and souvenirs from a number of the battles in which he took part, like the table made from the timbers of the Spanish fighting ship *San Josef* from the Battle of Cape St. Vincent, and the masthead of the French flagship *L'Orient* destroyed at the Battle of the Nile. Pride of place goes to Nelson's personal items, including his queue, knife and fork set, and the bloodstained uniform in which he died at the Battle of Trafalgar.

The Battle of Trafalgar marked the beginning of a century in which the Royal Navy was not called upon to fight any major sea battles, though it was kept busy dealing with pirates and slavers, as well as protecting trade routes and assisting, when necessary, the army in its colonial wars. The nineteenth century was a period of considerable innovation and development in naval warfare, as ships changed from the wooden sailing ships of Nelson's fleet, which were armed with cannon and still resembled in most respects the naval vessels of King Henry VIII, to the iron steamships with breech-loading guns that made up the fleet in 1900. The museum's 'Neptune Gallery' looks at these developments, mainly through the use of ship models, while its '20th Century Seapower' gallery examines, through static displays, video walls and interactives, the part played by the Royal Navy in the many conflicts this century.

The emphasis throughout the museum is on ships and how they were handled. The men who sailed them tend to be anonymous, except for their leaders, who are highlighted through their many portraits and personal items. It is little wonder that Kenneth Hudson (1987:119) was prompted to observe that 'anyone who studies Britain's National Maritime Museum at Greenwich objectively will quickly perceive that, in those sections devoted to the navy, what he is in fact looking at is a museum of the British Naval Officer in which ratings are little more than theatrical props, accessories to the main story'. The common seamen do make brief appearances, however, through, for instance, examples of their handicrafts shown in the 'Neptune Gallery', and in the many paintings of ships and naval actions which illustrate each historical period. Moreover, seamen's lives are described in some detail in the museum's guide, *The Story of Britain and the Sea*, and the museum archive contains examples of letters, diaries and other personal papers, as well as an enormous collection of books, ships' plans, paintings, prints and photographs. On the whole, however, those seeking depictions of the social history of the sailor need to look elsewhere.

The Royal Naval Museum

As I have said, the portrayal of that particular aspect of British naval history is not a stated objective of the National Maritime Museum. However, the Royal Naval Museum, Portsmouth, claims that it does 'concentrate on the people of the Royal Navy: ordinary sailors as well as officers' (White 1989:21). It is not, of course, a national museum, though the MGC Working Party Report did suggest that it might be sensible to form a federal 'National Museums of the Navy', incorporating the four designated naval museums, the Royal Naval Museum, the Royal Marines Museum, the Royal Navy Submarine Museum and the Fleet Air Arm Museum (MGC 1990:19). I have included it here because its collections have the range and scope of the national military museums, and it nicely complements both the National Maritime Museum and the National Army Museum.

In 1922 the Society for Nautical Research decided to preserve and restore HMS *Victory* to her Trafalgar condition. This prompted a small flood of donations of Nelson relics and other memorabilia which helped persuade the Society's Council that it would also need a museum close to the ship. An eighteenth-century rigging house opposite the *Victory* was converted, and the Victory Museum was opened in 1938, though it did not receive its first full-time curator until 1953, and it ran with only two uniformed ratings and one civilian warder until the early 1970s.

The Museum's collection continued to grow. Its oldest component was the collection of ships' figureheads, models and other artifacts from the Dockyard Museum at Portsmouth, which had originally opened in 1911. To this were added the historic artifacts from HMS *Victory*'s own small museum and two collections relating to the Royal Navy at the time of Nelson. One was donated by Mrs M.S. Ward, whose husband was the last of Nelson's great-grandsons, and consisted of personal items of Lord Nelson and Lady Hamilton. The second was given by an American, Mrs John McCarthy, and contained paintings, prints, pottery and other commemorative items relating to Lord Nelson. The additional artifacts were held in a number of different homes within the dockyard until the Royal Navy made available three Georgian storehouses adjacent to the Victory Museum. The MoD took over responsibility for the collection and set up the Royal Naval Museum in 1973 (Pack 1973:21). In 1975 the Douglas-Morris Collection of naval medals and memorabilia was also acquired, and this necessitated the establishment of a long-term development plan to house and display all this material, which culminated in 1987 in the present arrangement of the Museum's galleries. Meanwhile in 1984 under the National Heritage Act the Royal Naval Museum and the three other naval museums were devolved, and now receive their MoD support in the form of grant-in-aid, which covers part of their staff and operating costs (MGC 1990:19).

Clearly the Royal Naval Museum could be seen as the naval equivalent of the National Army Museum, telling the story of the Royal Navy for the general public. The nature of the collections at its disposal mean, however, that it has to be a slightly different sort of story. As we have already seen, life at sea did not allow the same kind of accumulation of artifacts that life in the army did. The emphasis in the Royal Naval Museum is, therefore, by necessity, much more on the craft and technology of sailing than on the individual lives of sailors, though it uses captions and graphic panels to fill in some of the gaps in the military and social history.

The museum's displays begin with a series of graphic panels which set the collection within its historical context by briefly recounting the history of the Royal Navy and explaining the rating of ships. Ship models and other artifacts illustrate the early history of the navy, and documents are used to good effect in relevant cases to show how ships were fitted out and made ready for sea. Manuscript letters are also used to describe life at sea at the time of the Battle of Trafalgar, and, in 'The Heyday of Fighting Ships' gallery, life in Nelson's navy is illustrated with examples of the tools of the sailors' trade, prints showing them at work and play and captions discussing their wages, the ship's hierarchy, recruitment, and crime and punishment. A later section on the Victorian navy shows examples of sailors' handicrafts, games and songs; except in these sections, there are relatively few artifacts belonging to common seamen on display.

The personal touch is supplied by the material pertaining to senior officers at different periods in naval history. Interesting insights into life at sea can be gleaned from the furniture and other effects of these admirals, though, of course, their personal equipment would have been of a vastly superior quality to that of the common seaman.

The fullest collection of such material relates to Admiral Lord Nelson. It was, after all, private collections of Nelson memorabilia which made up a large part of the original holdings of this museum. A number of personal items are on display, including his uniform and navigation tools and some poignant artifacts which show how he coped with having only one arm. There are also several objects and documents relating to his family life and to his famous liaison with Emma Hamilton. This is a rare glimpse of the sexual relations of a British hero; by emphasizing in the display the love and devotion between Nelson and his mistress, the scandalous nature of the affair is nevertheless played down.

Another interesting aspect of the Nelson story is the hagiography which surrounded him during his life and even more after his death. The museum's holdings, like those of the National Maritime Museum, contain a number of pieces of commemorative china and silver depicting Nelson's many victories and his hero's death. Similar mementos of other admirals are also on display in the museum, and give modern visitors an insight into the way in which military heroes were regarded and fêted in the early nineteenth century.

Like the National Maritime Museum, the Royal Naval Museum examines the nineteenth century mainly in terms of the developments which took place in ship and weapons design, and the way in which this affected naval operations. It does, however, place more emphasis on the 'policing' role the navy undertook throughout the world, and mentions its involvement in the many colonial wars of the period. The displays in the Victorian section also discuss the way these technical developments changed the lives of the seamen, and introduced both a greater professionalism in their training and a number of new specialist trades for which they could be trained. But once again much of this has to be shown by the use of graphic panels.

Overall the museum paints a broad picture of the Royal Navy in the period under review. It has on show detailed material about the ships and the way in which they were sailed, and examines the life and work of the sailors as much as it can. It also has a substantial archive of books, manuscripts, pictures, audio-visual material and photographs covering various aspects of the social, technological and operational history of the Royal Navy, as well as its reserve collection of artifacts which can be used by researchers. And it prides itself on providing an extensive educational service to adults and children.

The story the museum tells is reinforced by the two historic Royal Navy ships which lie in dry dock nearby. HMS *Victory* is the last remaining example of the 'wooden walls of England', and a visit to this ship can demonstrate more clearly than any amount of words or paintings what it must have been like to work, eat and sleep in one of the crowded lower decks of these late eighteenth- and early nineteenth-century ships-of-the-line. The effect is claustrophobic enough in dry dock, but with a little imagination a visitor may be able to envisage life at sea during a storm, or in the middle of a battle. Perhaps in time some entrepreneur will establish a 'Victory experience' which will allow visitors to experience the rolling of the ship, the sounds of gunfire and the screams of dying men, during the Battle of Trafalgar. But for the moment the sensation of being on this historic ship must suffice!

Nearby is moored HMS *Warrior*, a Royal Navy ironclad from the latter half of the nineteenth century, which is now an independent museum. This shows the way in which ship construction and weaponry had advanced between the beginning of the century, when the wooden HMS *Victory* was the main naval gun platform, and the 1860s, when iron ships, more closely resembling modern warships, were starting to emerge. A trip below decks suggests, however, that relatively little had changed in the living conditions of the ordinary seaman in those years.

Both these ships therefore provide a graphic illustration of the themes covered by the Royal Naval Museum. Without them visitors to the Museum might find it difficult to visualize what life at sea would have been like. Moreover, the Museum is located within a site of historic interest, which also includes the *Mary Rose* and the Mary Rose Museum and a Dockyard Exhibition describing the way ships were made and repaired. A visitor to this complex, therefore, has access to 400 years of naval history (Thomas 1994:16).

Clearly all these national museums present a very full history of Britain's armed forces and of the conflicts in which they have been engaged. But what overall picture emerges from their displays of service life before the twentieth century? It seems that none of the museums concentrate on presenting such a picture. They are, after all, expected to cover a lot of ground in a relatively small space. The National Army Museum and the Royal Naval Museum are possibly also partly constrained by being the official public faces of the two services, and have to balance telling the story of the servicemen, warts and all, against a natural inclination to trumpet their achievements and those of the forces they serve. But given the nature of the available artifacts, it is hardly surprising that the National Army Museum and the Scottish United Services Museum are able in fact to paint a more detailed portrait of the life of the soldier than the naval museums can provide for that of their servicemen.

On the other hand, the picture of the sailor's craft which emerges from the Royal Naval Museum and the National Maritime Museum is arguably fuller and more satisfying than the depiction of the soldier's profession which is visible in the displays of the other two nationals. Without the regimental and corps museums the description of the work of the army available to museum visitors would be a narrow one. On the other hand, the national museums dealing with the army cover, as one might expect, a much broader sweep than any single regimental or corps museum can, and they tackle topics with which these other museums are unable or unwilling to deal. To achieve all that might be expected of them, and, in particular, to present a more complete picture of the full range of activities and achievements of the army, would require far larger buildings and greater resources than the present national museums have at their disposal. Therefore, the national museums will have to continue to coexist with the regimental and corps museums if a complete picture of army life and activities is to be presented to the public.

Alternatively, Sir David Wilson (1992:83) has argued that the specialist national museums 'have a function which is probably more important than their displays in that they provide high level academic and technical support for a superstructure of scholarship which serves both the national and international community'. This is obviously applicable in these cases. These museums provide expert advice for other military museums' curators, and all four of these national museums (and the Royal Naval Museum) have substantial archival and reserve collections which are regularly consulted by military historians, authors, students and other researchers. Their curators also complement the displays with published guides which reflect their research into the museums' collections. Some extend this work to provide articles for scholarly journals and books on their field of expertise. It may well be that, in the present economic climate, less of their time is being spent on such scholarly activities than in the past, but the sheer size of these national institutions allows staff more facilities to extend the bounds of knowledge in their field than are available to the regimental and corps museum curators.

The position of national museums in the vanguard of research is uncontroversial. But in recent years some museologists have begun to debate the ultimate aim of the national military museums. The debate centres on the responsibility of these national museums to tackle the broader and deeper issues relating to military history, such as the morality of war and the interrelationship between the armed forces and the rest of society. Stephen Wood, for example, has argued that while it is to be expected that regimental museums will concentrate on the history and achievements of their own units to the exclusion of general discussions of the causes and effects of particular wars, national military museums do not have such an excuse. They must perforce be, he says, 'the most harshly political of museums. They exist to interpret the unacceptable side of foreign and domestic policy . . . ' and ought to act as the reflectors of the history of the nation's political decisions, without glossing over details or omitting unpalatable truths (Wood

1987b:65). It is, he believes, 'one of the most important functions of national military museums . . . to prevent present and future generations from committing the mistakes of the past . . . by illustrating them in a realistic and understandable way, that is in direct contrast to the unreal and vulgar representations churned out by the denizens of Hollywood'. But this, he argues, should not involve a political stance, but one of 'unvarnished, unglamorised, dispassionate realism, with objects used to illustrate their context and their part in the story of Man, and Woman, the Serviceman' (Wood 1987b:66).

He also wonders whether or not national military museums should involve themselves in dissecting the reasons why particular wars began and in trying to decide whether they were just or unjust wars, though he suggests that, in general, national museums, unsurprisingly, have tended to reflect the establishment view of national military policy (Wood 1986b:23). Yet he believes that in these post-colonial days it may just be possible to hint that, for example, in the past, the government had provoked colonial wars in order to increase the imperial domain (Wood 1986b:24). Whether this kind of comment can be made while these museums still enjoy a substantial amount of public funding is a moot point.

Stephen Wood suggests that the national museums could discuss the causes, effects and justice of past wars, while Kenneth Hudson (1991:17) argues, as was noted in Chapter 7, that they should include displays which show the impact that the military has had on society as a whole. Both of these men are suggesting changes in the role of the national military museums which go further than just redesigning their displays to show more of the daily life of the ordinary serviceman. They seem to be arguing that these museums should play a more central role in the interpretation of the military, social and political history of this country, rather than just augmenting the rather celebratory one played by the regimental museums. On the other hand, others, including Colonel Peter Walton would argue fiercely against any military museum, including the service-sponsored nationals, having a responsibility for matters beyond the role of the armed forces, partly because these museums could not be regarded as dispassionate in the examination of these social and political issues[3].

It seems doubtful, in any case, in the present economic and political climate, that these museums will begin tackling the more controversial topics suggested by Wood and Hudson. They are likely instead to look towards adopting a more commercial approach to their activities. This may include tackling some potentially popular topics, like the place of women in military history, but it is unlikely to encompass explorations of such possibly divisive topics as the morality of colonialism or the use of state violence. In the next decade I would expect to see more interactive and audio-visual displays in national museums, but I would be surprised to encounter a discussion of the causes of the Boer War or an examination of the influence of the leading arms manufacturers on British foreign policy.

As we know, the future is uncertain for all museums. How these national military museums and their smaller regimental cousins are likely to survive and develop in the next few years will be considered in the final chapter.

Notes

1. The Royal Military Academy retained its own museum, the Royal Military Academy Sandhurst Collection, which holds material relating to officer-training and to the histories of the Royal Military Academy and the Royal Military College, as well as the personal effects of some of the officers who trained in those institutions.
2. *Society of Friends Newsletter*, Volume IV, Summer 1993, No 2, p.3.
3. Letter from Colonel Peter Walton to author, 7 February 1995.

10. The Way Forward?

Probably what is more crucial now, though, than the carrot of a wider audience, appreciating and comprehending what the museum has to offer, is the stick of market forces.

(S. Wilkinson and I. Hughes 1991:23)

As the Irishman says in the well-known joke about asking directions 'to get where you're going, you shouldn't be starting from here'. In a way that could be said to sum up the present plight of many military museums. In a political and economic climate largely hostile to all museums, this specialist group is trying to find a new role, a new audience, and the financial resources to enable its members to survive into the twenty-first century. The days when these museums could flourish simply by telling the story of the glorious achievements of their particular unit to an audience of old comrades and military enthusiasts, while supported solely by the MoD and contributions from unit funds, are apparently over. The armed forces are shrinking. Some army regiments are disappearing, and their museums are being left out on a limb. The proportion of ex-servicemen in our population is diminishing, and the younger generation is no longer taught history through an examination of great leaders and great wars. Meanwhile the MoD is being forced to trim its budgets and to concentrate its resources on providing an efficient and cost-effective national defence. Military museums, it seems, have to find a new relevance or perish.

A new role does appear, in fact, to be beckoning to them. Since the 1980s new social history museums have emerged, exploring a variety of themes such as labour history, urban history, women's history or agricultural history. There is clearly a place for military history here, not, as in the past, merely as a record of battles and campaigns, but instead as a medium for examining the lives of those men and women who served in the armed forces, or who were touched in some other way by the military machine. Such an approach, many argue, can make military museums and the story they have to tell relevant to all parts of the next generation of museum visitors, and not just to the older men who have traditionally patronized them (Wilkinson and Hughes 1991:23). Perhaps this would then ensure that these museums have a permanent place in the museum provision of this country.

This social history function does seem to offer a way forward for military museums, and many are already moving in that direction. But here we have to return to the irony of the Irishman's advice, because for a number of reasons military museums are not perfectly suited to becoming another form of social history museum. Neither their collections nor their own history are ideal foundations for this new role, and the metamorphosis from the creature they are now to the one many argue they need to become will not be a painless, or, I suspect, a totally successful process.

In the first place, unlike many museums, they did not begin with collections which had been formed by learned men and women, using the scientific or artistic principles of their day, to create a treasure-house of specimens from which to research and draw scholarly conclusions. On the whole, military collections were originally formed by accident, or through a combination of looting, obsolescence and the accumulation of both trophies of war and personal souvenirs. These collections were then further refined, by either the exigencies of service life, or by their use as decorative features in a mess. Finally, the artifacts which made up these collections were selected or rejected as suitable items for their museums by men who held a particular view on the meaning of military history, and on the purpose which military museums should serve.

It is little wonder that the social history of service life that military museums tell for the historical period covered by this survey is such a patchy one. Moreover, messes, those essential intermediaries in the development of regimental museums, did not exist before the end of the eighteenth century, and it would be a rare family of a common soldier or sailor, that could afford the space needed to preserve a souvenir for 250 years. It is not surprising, therefore, that artifacts for the first hundred years of the period studied here are few, and of little help in constructing a social history of military life. Weapons and uniforms from that period do survive, but few of the common or personal items exist which would enable a museum to present a rounded picture of service life in that time. Ironically, the finds from the *Mary Rose* mean that a better display can be mounted relating to military life in the sixteenth century than could be achieved for the seventeenth or early eighteenth centuries by most military museums, if they used only original material.

The picture improves, of course, as we have seen, for later centuries, though before the middle of the nineteenth century displays of original artifacts have, by necessity, to be dominated by the possessions of officers. Moreover, the nature of collecting favours the survival of the special and the exotic rather than the ordinary and mundane. Soldiers and sailors and their messes, therefore, were more likely to hold on to ethnographic material, war trophies or ceremonial uniforms, than ordinary pieces of equipment or other everyday items, like beds, blankets or brushes.

Other aspects of service life, such as the class divisions between officers and men, the purchase system, sexual relations, family life, faith and fear, amongst many other topics, are difficult to illustrate using artifacts. Military museums, including the Regiments of Gloucestershire Museum and the Royal Scots Regimental Museum which tackle such abstract topics, have to tread a fine line between conveying sufficient information on the one hand, and turning the museum into a book on the wall on the other.

The national museums have the breadth of collections to enable them to make a good attempt at telling the social history of service life, but for the regimental and corps museums, as I have suggested, the practical problems are much greater. They also have to change the whole ethos and philosophy of their museums to move in this new direction, and this can often be a painful process for all concerned. Christine Beresford has admitted (Beresford 1991:27) that, in planning the redevelopment of the Regiments of Gloucestershire Museum, the 'omissions and inclusions made were not all popular with the regiment', and the redesign of the Museum of the Manchesters irritated at least one traditionalist (Preece 1987:71), though I suspect there were many other critics who were less vocal.

These museums were originally set up, after all, with the intention of achieving very different aims. Their collections had been taken out of the messes and private homes, and then brought together into a museum, primarily as a way of demonstrating the heritage and achievements of the particular unit to its own recruits and to the general public, at a time when making these achievements and traditions concrete and public might help both to preserve them and to prolong the life of the unit. Moreover little changed in the next 50 years to nullify or alter these original aims. Indeed, it should be remembered that the armed forces, which still largely fund the majority of these military museums, have a continuing need to encapsulate their history and traditions and to present them to both recruits, servicemen and women and the general public through their museums, and that these museums, which the MGC observed (MGC 1990:42) were 'a quintessential part' of the fabric of the services, cannot totally forget or ignore their recruiting, training and public relations roles.

It is small wonder then that telling the story of the ordinary soldier or sailor was not (and is often still not) high on their list of priorities. It could be argued, however, that the basis for such a story has always been there. Ships, regiments, corps and other military units pride themselves on being proto-families, and so, while they emphasize the achievements of the family as a whole, they do not ignore its individual members. The medal galleries of naval, regimental and corps museums are only the most obvious way in which the achievements and sacrifices of individual family members are remembered and lauded. But, in general, in the past the whole was seen to be greater than the sum of its parts, and the balance of the displays reflected, therefore, the story of the unit rather than that of its individual members.

Moreover, not only was the story the one of the unit rather than that of the individual; the best part of the story tended to be told. A regiment or ship could be defeated, but in defeat the men had to be shown to be brave and resolute. Far better to celebrate the victories and the achievements. There was no place here to ask the awkward questions about the way soldiers or sailors were recruited, how much they were paid, how they were treated or what happened to them when they finished their service. It was not that these questions were deliberately ignored, or that lies were told, it was just that their consideration had no part in the story.

But it is impossible to tell the social history of service life without tackling subjects like pay, rations, living conditions, crime and punishment, family life, class divisions, disease and death. An accurate picture of military history cannot be drawn without discussing defeats, corruption and ineptitude as well as victories, successes, courage and skill. And the examination of such topics cannot fail to show some aspects of service life in earlier centuries, and also, possibly, certain past members of the particular unit or service, in a very poor light.

Many of these museums no longer represent living regiments, and, in most cases, the recruiting function of those museums which are connected with current units may not now be considered to be a major role. But their trustees are usually drawn from those who have served in the particular unit. It is to be expected that they would still wish to preserve its traditions and good name, and they might find it hard to accept changes in emphasis within the museum which seemed to present a darker picture of military history, or perhaps played down the glorious achievements of the unit, in favour of presenting the more mundane aspects of military life. It is to the credit of the trustees of some museums, such as those of the Regiments of Gloucestershire Museum, that they have accepted that a new balance has to be struck in the themes portrayed in the museum. It is clear that others are merely waiting to acquire the funds to carry out similar radical changes.

In fact a number of regimental and corps museums now describe the social conditions under which their soldiers lived and fought and point to the interaction between their unit and the civilian population. However, in most cases this constitutes only a small part of the story, and the main emphasis is still on telling of the battles fought and won and of the achievements of the unit in all fields. Indeed, as I argued in Chapter 5, there would be little point in keeping these museums if they all told a very similar story of the daily lives of their servicemen and totally lost sight of their unique history. Nevertheless, the social history element of their story is an important one and in many cases a start has been made in telling it.

The museums of the Royal Navy may not seem at first glance to place great emphasis in their displays on telling the social history of the sailor. The National Maritime Museum is not in any real sense a military museum and so cannot be expected to look at the Royal Navy sailor's lot in any great detail, but the Royal Naval Museum, which is, does focus more on the social history of the sailor. As it explains, however, the nature of life at sea meant that relatively few relevant artifacts from the common sailor have come into the Museum's possession. Both museums, as we have seen, display a number of the personal belongings of Nelson and of other senior naval figures, but these are by definition not ordinary or representative of the life of the common seaman, though, of course, the life of the officer is as much a part of the social history of service life as that of the ordinary soldier or sailor. These museums do, however, also show examples of sailors' handicrafts, and describe their work and their living conditions in some detail through illustrated captions and in their museum publications. This material forms a useful introduction to the social history of the sailor, while the few remaining historic ships help to show what life must have been like below decks for the officers and men in the Georgian and Victorian navies.

On the whole, though, as was noted in Chapter 9, the naval museums concentrate on telling another, equally valid, part of the story of life at sea: that of the art and craft of sailing. Sailing in general, and naval warfare in particular, is a highly technical subject, using, in the naval ship, a complex machine in a potentially hostile and taxing environment. These museums show us how these ships were designed, built, navigated and fought, and how naval tactics and techniques developed through time. They try, with the artifacts at their disposal, to juxtapose this technical story against both the history of naval warfare and the lives of the men who made all these achievements possible.

The picture is changing, therefore, and the ordinary men and women are starting to emerge from the general military background to stare back at us from the glass cases and challenge our perceptions of what military history is all about. More needs to be done, of course, particularly in showing how the armed forces related to the civilian population. But on the whole, military museums seem to be shaking off their past and to be taking note of the way other social history museums in this country are beginning to display their story. Moreover, they are increasingly drawing on the experience and expertise of museum designers who have worked in the broader museum field to help them refurbish their displays and make them more relevant to future generations of museum visitors.

But military museums, particularly the smaller regimental and corps museums, will not solve all their problems by simply changing the emphasis of their displays. Many of them are still situated in unsuitable buildings with inadequate visitor facilities, and are sited within army camps which are either a long way from centres of civilization and tourism, or surrounded by intimidating security fences, or both. Moreover, as is all too painfully clear in some cases, they still often have insufficient trained staff to look after their collections adequately, let alone provide the educational and customer care services expected of a modern museum. And above all they lack the financial resources to make the necessary improvements. The future of some of these museums looks bleak, unless they can find the professional assistance, and the funds, to improve their operations and facilities, and thereby attract more visitors.

Their problems may, in fact, be compounded if the MoD is unable to maintain the same level of funding to its museums that it has provided for the last 30 years, because of mounting Treasury and political pressure to make cuts in its budget and to concentrate its resources on providing the best possible front-line defence forces. It is becoming increasingly clear to MoD-maintained museums (and this may well apply equally to local authority military museums in the face of rate-capping and the massive local government reorganization), that they will have to generate an ever-increasing proportion of the funds they need to cover their running costs. That is forcing them to question what they do and how they do it, and it is a far more fundamental review than just deciding whether or not to show barrack-room scenes and to adopt a clearer social history orientation. Their emphasis is shifting, by necessity, towards trying to find ways of attracting more people into the museum and then giving them an enjoyable time once they are there. A number of museums are placing their faith in the redesign of their galleries along conventional lines to accomplish this goal, but others are adopting very untraditional ways of achieving the same ends.

The new buzz-word is 'experience', and a few military museums are adopting some of the modern techniques available to the 'heritage industry' to liven up their displays. Both the Regiments of Gloucestershire Museum and the Royal Marines Museum, for example, use animated models to tell part of their story. The Regiments of Gloucestershire Museum, the Military Museum of Devon and Dorset, and a few other military museums also use interactive computers to enable the visitor to learn more about the history of the regiment, or to sample more of the museum's collection than can be shown in the galleries. The Royal Norfolk Regimental Museum has just such a programme which uses an illustration of the Battle of Vittorio in June 1813 as a touch-screen. Visitors may touch relevant parts of the picture to obtain information about the participants, the terrain, the tactics used and the importance of the battle, and in the process can learn about more general topics like camp followers and the functions of different army units. These machines undoubtedly do add to the experience that the visitor gains by going to the particular museum. But, of course, these automatons and computers are expensive, and each museum usually boasts only one or two alongside their more conventional displays.

Other museums, with more money and space, have introduced different machine-driven experiences. The Imperial War Museum, for example, has sights, sounds and smells in its First World War 'trench experience', and in its Second World War 'Blitz Experience' movement is added to the other effects. A few museums, including the Fleet Air Arm Museum, have introduced simulators, so that visitors, by sitting in a large box moved by hydraulic computer-guided jacks synchronized to an image projected onto a screen, can enjoy a simulated flight in an aircraft or a ride on a motorcycle. The Fleet Air Arm Museum has, in fact, combined a number of such experiences, to dramatic effect, in its new aircraft carrier exhibition.

A few military museums, however, are planning to go even further along the 'experience' road. The Royal Marines Museum, for instance, is intending to develop its site in Southsea to include a challenging assault course which visitors of all ages will be able to tackle, so that they can gain some insight into what it is like to train to be a Marine. There will also be a boating pond with small landing craft on it for the public to try, and other activities simulating the work of Marine Commandos. The whole idea is to add considerably to the enjoyment of a family group visiting the museum, while at the same time trying to demonstrate aspects of the life of a Marine which cannot adequately be conveyed in a static display.

But some military museum projects have been even more adventurous. As we saw in Chapter 6, Aldershot Garrison houses a number of separate military museums commemorating some of the smaller corps and specialist units stationed there[1]. Aldershot has also been, of course, the home of the British Army for 140 years, and a proposal has been put forward for combining in one site all these various military museums, together with the Aldershot Military Museum, which records this long association between the army and the garrison, to provide a more comprehensive history than any of the individual museums can achieve on their own.

If this scheme came to fruition, therefore, a visitor interested in military history would be able to see displays on both the history of the garrison and that of these corps, and of the Royal Aircraft Establishment, Farnborough, together in one place. This museum development, according to its promotional brochure, 'will show fighting achievements, logistics, medicine and intelligence, aviation and space technology. It will tell the story of soldiers, scientists and test pilots, agents and prisoners, as well as their families and civilians mobilised in war'.

That is a thoroughly sensible suggestion, but the project, called 'Challenge Aldershot', goes far beyond the mere collocation of these museums and their redisplay. It also aims at building a large complex with a cinema and visitor centre in which the customers will be able to learn about the British Army in general, and the work of the corps featured there in particular. These facilities would be available for other demonstrations as well.

After looking round the visitor centre the customer can go to the arena where various displays and activities would be taking place, or – and this is where 'Challenge Aldershot' finally moves away from the normal museum idea – the visitor might choose instead to become a participant. As the preliminary brochure states, 'it is now possible to simulate a parachute jump, or a cavalry charge, and set visitors tests of their skill and judgment similar to those faced by soldiers in the field and scientists on a test-bench'. Interactive videos would allow a historic narrative to be presented which breaks off at a crucial point and presents the viewers with choices for action. Once they have chosen, the video can continue showing them the consequences of their choice. In that way, design, logistics and intelligence problems can be modelled on the screen to be solved by the visitor (Tod 1991:25).

The problems of conveying the movement of war and of explaining the technical aspects of warfare can be overcome in part, therefore, by the use of simulators and audience participation techniques learned from the Disney Corporation. This, it is hoped, will allow visitors to appreciate the skills needed to be a modern soldier while at the same time giving them an enjoyable experience.

This project may fail because of the considerable amount of money that needs to be raised to realize it, though the burden of fundraising does not fall on the participating museums alone. It is, in fact, a joint venture between the local authority, anxious to encourage tourists to its area, and a private consortium consisting of both the trustees of the corps museums, who are trying to find a reliable source of future funding and visitors for their museums, and private developers who see the commercial possibilities of bringing the public into contact with this particular military experience.

Although a similar attempt, albeit on a more modest scale, at building such a consortium at the Portsmouth Dockyard failed, it did lead to a greater degree of cooperation between the different museums and historic ships on the site (Thomas 1994:16). This suggests that such joint projects, probably including commercial partners, may be a way forward for some military museums, as it has been for the development of the Chatham Historic Dockyard.

What effect this emphasis on visitor experience will have, however, on the way in which military history is displayed in military museums remains to be seen. The Regiments of Gloucestershire Museum, the Museum of the Manchesters, the new galleries in the National Army Museum and a number of the other new museum developments that we have studied here are encouraging for those who believe that military museums should mirror other social history museums in the way they tell the story of the men and women behind the events. But whether projects like 'Challenge Aldershot' will place the same emphasis on showing what life was really like in the armed forces for our ancestors, or whether, instead, they will concentrate more on accentuating certain aspects of military service, and in particular its glory and adventure, will become clear in time. It will also be interesting to see whether such 'experiences' prove to be better public relations tools for the armed forces than the museums which are adopting a social history bias.

There are other ways in which military museums can survive these difficult times. One suggestion, as we have seen in Chapter 7, is that these museums should combine on a county-wide basis (as has already taken place in a few cases (MGC 1990:25)), presumably with all the county's military museums on one local authority museum site, though with the collections still controlled by the regimental trusts. Whether this is economically or political viable will depend, I suspect, on the way in which the current round of local government reorganization turns out. I do not think the signs are encouraging at the moment, though in the long term it may be the only sensible solution to the problem of the maintenance of so many small regimental museums. It might also prevent the museums of defunct units being preserved predominantly as memorials to the regiment, as for example the Cameronians Regimental Museum was for 25 years[2], as that seems to me a potentially sterile and limited purpose for what are often interesting and historically valuable collections.

Such a scheme, however, might leave the corps museums out on a limb, because their parent units rarely have a strong local connection, despite having collections of national importance, and being acknowledged as playing an important training and educational role for the army (MGC 1990:23–4). There is no suggestion at the moment that the MoD will remove its support from these museums, though it may encourage them to raise a greater share of their running costs in the future. Indeed the recent MoD decisions concerning the museums it supports, reported at the end of Chapter 3, suggest that for the time being, at least, it will not attempt to change the status quo.

But the future is as uncertain for military museums as it is for most civilian museums. Museums are facing a new century in which their whole *raison d'être* is likely to be challenged. They have been accused in the last decade of being elitist, old-fashioned and irrelevant. The idea of showing artifacts in glass cases, in an age of television, interactive experiences and audience participation, seems to some people as unnecessary as showing wild animals in zoo cages; both may fall before the rival attractions offered by pseudo-Disneylands.

Military museums, moreover, may seem to have even further to go than their civilian cousins in the search for a relevant and secure future. They have been accused, after all, of being old-fashioned and irrelevant even by other members of their own profession! Kenneth Hudson, for example, has said that 'with each year that passes I find myself asking why this army or naval or air force museum is still there. What exactly is its purpose, now . . . ' (1991:17). He argues that equating history with international politics and military campaigns is now totally obsolete, though he seems to be in favour of keeping military museums if they tell us about 'the cost of wars, the cultural and social gap between the private soldier and his officers, the soldier as a member of society, the conflict between the military and the civil virtues, and the appalling human suffering and wastefulness of the whole dreadful business . . . ' These are, indeed, just the issues that military museums are beginning to tackle, albeit slowly.

On the other hand, whether we like it or not, this country has had a long and important military history which deserves to be recorded. Being a soldier or a sailor was as much a trade in the period I have examined as being a carpenter or a cooper, and our army and navy have played a substantial part in moulding our country and our society through their contribution to the formation and retention of the British Empire and their defence of the internal status quo. These topics may be unpalatable now, but they cannot and should not be ignored and swept aside if future generations are to have available a true picture of our history, warts and all.

For the present I hope this survey has shown that there is a rich diversity in the way the military history of the seventeenth, eighteenth and nineteenth centuries is shown in our museums. Many of the displays are still old-fashioned and largely uninformative, with the emphasis on showing the glorious achievements of a particular unit while ignoring the realities of warfare and of the lives of the men and women involved. Yet trustees, curators and designers are increasingly realizing that they have a richer story to tell, and are putting common, and not so common, men and women into the galleries and telling their stories, along with those of the units in which they spent so much of their lives. From being the most backward and old-fashioned, many of these new displays are incorporating interpretative features, such as tableaux, animated figures, interactive videos and simulators, which are in advance of what many similar social history museums are using.

I fervently believe that military museums are an essential part of the museum provision in this country, and it would be a tragedy if they were allowed to disappear. But I am optimistic that the spirit which originally brought these museums into existence, and which has sustained them through many difficult times in the past, will help at least some of them to survive in the future. Indeed the signs are not all gloomy. New projects for refurbishing regimental museums are appearing even in these difficult times. Fundraising is currently under way for major redevelopments for, amongst others, the museums of the Royal Scots Dragoon Guards and of the King's Own Royal Regiment. These refurbishments are intended to incorporate modern design techniques which, as the appeal brochure of the King's Own Royal Regiment Museum claims, will be used to add 'a social history element to complement the military history and proud history of the regiment'. They will also allow 'visitors with a general interest to gain an insight into the role and significance of the regiment'. It is intended that this redisplay, like the others planned elsewhere, will 'ensure its continued success into the 21st Century'. I, too, hope that it will succeed as the story these museums have to tell is too important to lose.

Notes

1. These included (before the recent formation of the Royal Logistic Corps and the subsequent amalgamation of its component units' museums) the museums of the Airborne Forces, the Army Catering Corps, the Army Physical Training Corp, the Queen Alexandra's Royal Army Nursing Corps, the Royal Army Dental Corps, the Royal Army Veterinary Corps, the Regimental Museum of the Royal Corps of Transport and the Royal Army Medical Corps Historical Museum.
2. Letter to author, 25 November 1994, from Elizabeth Hancock, Keeper of Collections, Hamilton District Council Cultural Services.

Appendix: List of Military Museums

This is not an exhaustive list of military museums and museums with military collections but includes those which are accessible to the public without a prior appointment. A complete catalogue of relevant museums, with locations and opening times, is available in the excellent work, *A Guide to Military Museums and Other Places of Military Interest*, written and published by Terence and Shirley Wise.

This table lists museums alphabetically and shows the other major regimental collections each particular museum holds which are not indicated by its title.

Airborne Forces Museum	Parachute Regiment, Glider Pilot Regiment
Aldershot Military Museum	
Army Physical Training Corps Museum	Army Physical Training Staff
Aryshire Yeomanry Museum	
Bedford Museum	Bedfordshire Yeomanry
Bedfordshire and Hertfordshire Regimental Museum	16th (Bedfordshire) Regiment of Foot
Blackburn Museum and Art Gallery	30th (Cambridgeshire), 59th (2nd Nottinghamshire) Foot, East Lancashire Regiment
Black Watch Museum	42nd and 73rd Foot
Blair Castle	Atholl Highlanders
Border Regiment and Kings Own Royal Border Regiment Museum	34th (Cumberland), 55th (Westmorland) Foot
Buffs Regimental Museum	3rd Foot, Royal East Kent Regiment
Cannon Hall Museum and Art Gallery	13th/18th Royal Hussars
Cheshire Military Museum	5th Royal Inniskilling Dragoon Guards, 3rd Carabiniers, 22nd (Cheshire) Regiment, Cheshire Yeomanry

Coldstream Museum	Lord General's Regiment of Foot, Coldstream Guards
Duke of Cornwall's Light Infantry Regimental Museum	32nd (Cornwall), 46th (South Devonshire) Foot
Duke of Wellington's Regimental Museum	33rd, 76th Foot
Durham Light Infantry Museum and Arts Centre	68th (Durham Light Infantry) Foot, 106th (Bombay Light Infantry), Militia and Volunteers
Essex Regiment Museum	44th (East Sussex), 56th (West Sussex) Foot
Fleet Air Arm Museum	Royal Naval Air Service
Fort Nelson Museum of Artillery	
Fusiliers Museum of Northumberland	5th Foot, Royal Northumberland Fusiliers
Gordon Highlanders Regimental Museum	75th, 92nd (Gordon Highlanders) Foot
Green Howards Museum	19th Foot, Alexandra, Princess of Wales's Own Yorkshire Regiment, North York Militia and Volunteers
Guards Museum	Grenadier, Coldstream, Scots, Irish, Welsh Guards
Gurkha Museum	
Hereford Regiment and Hereford Light Infantry Museum	36th (Herefordshire), 29th (Worcestershire) Foot
Hertford Museum	49th Hertford Regiment
Hertfordshire Yeomanry and Artillery Historical Trust Museum	
Household Cavalry Museum	1st and 2nd Life Guards, Horse Grenadier Guards, Royal Horse Guards, 1st Royal Dragoons, Blues and Royals
Imperial War Museum	
Intelligence Corps Museum	
John George Joicey Museum	15th/19th The King's Royal Hussars, Northumberland

John George Joicey Museum (cont)	Hussars, 15th The King's Hussars, 19th Royal Hussars (Queen Alexandra's Own)
Kent Sharpshooters Yeomanry Museum	East Kent Yeomanry, West Kent Yeomanry, 3rd/4th County of London Yeomanry
King's Own Royal Regiment (Lancaster) Museum	4th Foot, 1st Royal Lancashire Militia
King's Own Scottish Borderers Regimental Museum	25th Foot
King's Own Yorkshire Light Infantry Regimental Gallery, Doncaster Museum	51st Foot, 105th (Madras Light Infantry), 1st West York Yeomanry Cavalry, Yorkshire Dragoons, York and Lancaster Regiment
Lancashire County and Regimental Museum	30th, 40th, 47th, 59th, 81st, 82nd Foot, Queen's Lancashire Regiment, 14th/20th King's Hussars, Duke of Lancaster's Own Yeomanry, Lancashire Hussars Yeomanry
Light Infantry Museum	King's Own Yorkshire, Somerset and Cornwall, King's Shropshire, and Durham Light Infantry
Loughborough War Memorial Museum	Leicestershire Yeomanry
Mary Rose Museum	
Military Museum of Devon and Dorset	11th, 39th Foot, Devonshire Regiment, Dorsetshire Regiment, Queen's Own Dorset Yeomanry, Militia and Volunteers
Muckleburgh Collection	Suffolk and Norfolk Yeomanry
Museum of Army Flying	Royal Flying Corps, Glider Pilot Regiment, Air Observation Post Squadron Royal Artillery
Museum of Army Transport	East Riding Yeomanry

Museum of Artillery	Royal Artillery
Museum of the Duke of Edinburgh's Royal Regiment	49th, 62nd, 66th, 99th Foot, Royal Berkshire and Wiltshire Regiment, Militia and Volunteers
Museum of the King's Regiment (Liverpool)	8th Foot
Museum of Lincolnshire Life	10th (North Lincolnshire) Foot, Royal Lincolnshire Regiment, Lincolnshire Yeomanry
Museum of the Manchesters	63rd, 96th Foot, Manchester Regiment
Museum of the Northamptonshire Regiment	48th, 58th (Rutlandshire) Foot
Museum of North Devon	Royal Devon Yeomanry
Museum of the Royal Army Chaplains' Department	
Museum of the Royal Highland Fusiliers	21st (Royal North British) Foot, Princess Margaret's Own Glasgow and Ayrshire Regiment, Royal Scots Fusiliers
Museum of the Royal Leicestershire Regiment	17th Foot
Museum of the Staffordshire Regiment (The Prince of Wales's)	38th, 64th, 80th, 98th Foot
Museum of the Staffordshire Yeomanry (Queen's Own Royal Regiment)	
National Army Museum	Irish Regiments, Imperial Indian Army Regiments, Middlesex Regiment, Women's Royal Army Corps.
Newhaven Military Museum	Queen's Regiment
Pembroke Yeomanry Trust	Militia, Volunteers
Powysland Museum and Montgomery Canal Centre	Montgomeryshire Yeomanry Cavalry
Prince of Wales's Own Regiment of Yorkshire Museum	14th (Buckinghamshire), 15th Foot, West Yorkshire Regiment, East Yorkshire Regiment

Princess of Wales's Royal Regiment and Queen's Regimental Museum	Buffs, East Surrey, Royal Sussex, Royal Hampshire, Queen's Own Royal West Kent, and Middlesex Regiments
Queen Alexandra's Royal Army Nursing Corps Museum	Army Nursing Reserve, Queen Alexandra's Imperial Military Nursing Service
Queen's Own Royal West Kent Regiment Museum	50th, 97th (Earl of Ulster's) Foot, Militia, 20th London, Kent Cyclists
Queen's Royal Surrey Regiment Museum	31st (Huntingdonshire), 70th (Surrey), East Surrey Regiment, Queen's Royal Regiment
RAF Regiment Museum	
Regiments of Gloucestershire Museum	28th, 161st Foot, Gloucestershire Regiment, Royal Gloucestershire Hussars
Regimental Museum, Argyll and Sutherland Highlanders	91st, 93rd Foot
Regimental Museum, The Cameronians	26th (Cameronian) Foot, 90th Perthshire Light Infantry, Scottish Rifles
Regimental Museum XX The Lancashire Fusiliers	20th (East Devonshire) Foot
Regimental Museum Oxfordshire and Buckinghamshire Light Infantry	43rd (Monmouthshire Light Infantry), 52nd (Oxfordshire Light Infantry)
Regimental Museum 1st The Queen's Dragoon Guards	1st King's Dragoon Guards, Queen's Bays
Regimental Museum, Queen's Lancashire Regiment	30th, 59th Foot, 40th, 82nd, 47th, 81st Foot, East Lancashire, South Lancashire, North Lancashire Regiments
Regimental Museum of Queen's Own Highlanders	72nd, 78th, 79th Foot, Seaforth Highlanders, Queen's Own Cameron Highlanders, Lovat Scouts

Regimental Museum of the Queen's Own Hussars	3rd King's Own Hussars, 7th Queen's Own Hussars
Regimental Museum of the Royal Inniskilling Fusiliers	27th (Inniskilling), 108th (Madras Infantry) Foot
Regimental Museum The Royal Irish Fusiliers	87th, 89th Foot, Militia
Regimental Museum of the 9th/12th Royal Lancers (Prince of Wales's)	95th Foot, Derbyshire Regiment, Derbyshire Yeomanry
Regimental Museum The Royal Welch Fusiliers	23rd Foot
Regimental Museum of the South Wales Borderers and Monmouthshire Regiment of the Royal Regiment of Wales	24th (2nd Warwickshire) Foot
REME Museum	
Royal Air Force Museum	Royal Engineers Balloon Units, Royal Flying Corps, Royal Naval Air Service
Royal Army Dental Corps Historical Museum	
Royal Army Educational Corps Museum	Corps of Army Schoolmasters
Royal Army Medical Corps Historical Museum	Medical Staff Corps
Royal Army Pay Corps Museum	Army Pay Department
Royal Army Veterinary Corps Museum	
Royal Artillery Regimental Museum	
4th/7th Royal Dragoon Guards Museum	
Royal Engineers Museum	Royal Sappers and Miners
Royal Green Jackets Museum	43rd, 52nd Foot, Oxfordshire and Buckinghamshire Light Infantry, King's Royal Rifle Corps, Rifle Brigade
Royal Hampshire Regiment Museum	37th, 67th Foot
Royal Hospital Museum	
Royal Hussars Museum	10th, 11th Royal Hussars

Royal Logistic Corps Museum	Royal Corps of Transport, Royal Army Ordnance Corps, Royal Pioneer Corps, Army Catering Corps, Postal and Courier Service Royal Engineers
Royal Marines Museum	
Royal Military Police Museum	Military Mounted Police, Military Foot Police
Royal Monmouthshire Royal Engineers (Militia) Museum	
Royal Naval Museum	
Royal Navy Submarine Museum	
Royal Norfolk Regimental Museum	9th (East Norfolk) Foot
Royal Regiment of Fusiliers (City of London) Museum	7th Foot
Royal Scots Dragoon Guards Museum	2nd Dragoons, 3rd Carabiniers, Royal Scots Greys
Royal Scots Regimental Museum	1st Foot
Royal Signals Museum	Royal Engineer Signal Service, Middlesex Yeomanry
Royal Ulster Rifles Museum	83rd (County of Dublin), 86th (Royal County Down) Foot, Royal Irish Rifles
Royal Warwickshire Regimental Museum	6th Foot, Royal Warwickshire Fusiliers
Rutland County Museum	58th Foot, Rutland Volunteers
Saffron Walden Museum	Essex Regiment
Scottish Horse Museum	
Scottish United Services Museum	
Sherwood Foresters Museum	45th, 95th Foot, Nottinghamshire and Derbyshire Regiment
Shropshire Regimental Museum	Shropshire Light Infantry, Militia, Volunteers

Somerset Military Museum	13th Foot, Somerset Light Infantry, North Somerset Yeomanry, West Somerset Yeomanry, Militia and Volunteers
Suffolk Regimental Museum	12th (East Suffolk) Foot, 1st East Anglian Regiment, 1st Battalion Royal Anglian Regiment
Sussex Combined Services Museum	35th Foot, 107th Bengal Infantry, Royal Sussex Regiment, Queen's Royal Irish Hussars, Militia and Volunteers
Tank Museum	Royal Armoured Corps, Royal Tank Regiment
Tyne and Wear Museums	15th/19th King's Royal Husssars, Northumberland Hussars
Townsley Hall Art Gallery	3rd Battalion East Lancashire Regiment
Warwickshire Yeomanry Regiment Museum	
Welch Regiment of the Royal Regiment of Wales Museum	41st (The Welsh), 69th (South Lincolnshire) Foot, Militia, Volunteers
Westmorland and Cumberland Yeomanry Museum	
Worcestershire Regimental Museum	29th (Worcestershire), 36th (Herefordshire) Foot, Militia, Volunteers
Worcestershire Yeomanry Museum	
York and Lancaster Regimental Museum	65th (2nd Yorkshire), 84th York and Lancaster) Foot

Bibliography

Barnett, C. (1970), *Britain and Her Army 1509–1970: A Military, Political, and Social Survey*, London, Allen Lane The Penguin Press.

Barton, K. (1980), 'Museum collections in a changing world', *Museums Association Conference Proceedings*.

Bassett, D.A. (1993), 'Museum publications: a descriptive and bibliographical guide', in Fleming, D., Paine, C., and Rhodes, J.G., (eds), *Social History in Museums: A Handbook for Professionals*, London, HMSO.

Beresford, C. (1991), in 'Soldiering on', by S. Wilkinson and I. Hughes, *Museums Journal*, 91,11:27.

Boardman, R. (1990), 'Army museums move and merge', *Museums Journal*, 90,8:14.

Boultbee, H.L. (1951), 'Royal Military Academy, Sandhurst, Museum', *Museums Journal*, 51,1:16.

Boyden, P.B. (1987), 'Regimental Records of the British Army 1850–1900', *Army Museum '87*, London, National Army Museum.

Brown, A.W. (1960), 'The Tank Museum', *Museums Journal*, 60,3:75–7.

Conway, Sir M. (1920), 'The scope of the Imperial War Museum', *Museums Journal*, 20,2:17–28.

Conybeare, C. (1994), 'Many military museums face cuts in their supply lines', *Museums Journal*, 94,6:8–9.

Cousins, G. (1968), *The Defenders: A History of the British Volunteers*, London, Frederick Muller.

Cowper, L.I. (1935), 'British military museums', *Museums Journal*, 35,2:40–9.

De Watteville, H.G. (1954), *The British Soldier: His Daily Life from Tudor to Modern Times*, London, J.M. Dent & Sons Ltd.

Dickinson, R.J. (1973), *Officers' Mess*, Tunbridge Wells, Midas Books.

Dickson, W.K-L. (1901), *The Biograph in Battle: Its Story in the South African War Related with Personal Experiences*, (reprinted 1995), Trowbridge, Flicks Books.

ffoulkes, C.J. (1918), 'War Museums', *Museums Journal*,18,4:57–61.

Forty, G. (1987), 'The Tank Museum: A case study', *Museums Journal*, 87,2:73–5.

Frostick, E. (1993), 'Special Problems: Documents', in Fleming, D., Paine, C., and Rhodes, J.G., (eds), *Social History in Museums: A Handbook for Professionals*, London, HMSO.

Gernsheim, H. and A. (1971), *A Concise History of Photography*, London, Thames and Hudson.

Goldsmith, A. (1979), *The Camera and Its Images*, Ridge Press.

Green, O. (1993), 'Collecting methods: photographs, film and video', in Fleming, D., Paine, C., and Rhodes J.G., (eds), *Social History in Museums: A Handbook for Professionals*, London, HMSO.

Greene, M. (1991), 'Closure of army camps threatens army museums', *Museums Journal*, 91,10:13.

Griffin, D. (1985), *Encyclopaedia of Modern British Army Regiments*, Wellingborough, Patrick Stephens.

Hackett, J.W. (1962), *Profession of Arms*, London, The Times Publishing Company Ltd.

Harrington, P. (1993), *British Artists and War: The Face of Battle in Paintings and Prints 1700–1914*, London, Greenhill Books.

Heughan, S. (1934), 'The new museum of the King's Liverpool Regiment at Seaforth Barracks, Liverpool', *Museums Journal*, 34,8:423–4.

Howard, M. (1959), 'Introduction: the armed forces as a political problem', in Howard, M. (ed), *Soldiers and Governments: Nine Studies in Civil-Military Relations*, Bloomington, Indiana University Press.

Howard, M. (1976), *War in European History*, Oxford, Oxford University Press.

Howard, M. (1978), *War and the Liberal Conscience*, London, Temple Smith.

Hudson, K. (1983), 'Military Museums', *Illustrated London News*.

Hudson, K. (1987), *Museums of Influence*, Cambridge, Cambridge University Press.

Hudson, K. (1991), 'Letter from the Museum of the Army', *Museums Journal*, 91,11:17.

Hughes, B. (1975), 'The Museum of Artillery in the Rotunda at Woolwich', *Museums Journal*, 74,4:177–8.

Jones, M.E. (1979), 'The regimental museum the Welch Regiment', in *The Bulletin of the Military Historical Society*, XX1X, 115:82.

Kavanagh, G. (1984), 'Museums, memorials and minewerfers', *Museums Journal*, 84,2:65–9.

Kavanagh, G. (1993), 'History in museums: A brief survey of trends and ideas', in Fleming, D., Paine, C., and Rhodes J.G., (eds), *Social History in Museums: A Handbook for Professionals*, London, HMSO.

Kavanagh, G. (1994), *Museums and the First World War: A Social History*, London, Leicester University Press.

Kenyon, J.R. (1992), 'Museum Libraries', in Thompson, J.M.A. (ed), *Manual of Curatorship: A Guide to Museum Practice*, (2nd ed), Oxford, Butterworth Heinemann.

Lazenby, W.C. (1989), 'Museum interpretation of war and the military: an overview', unpublished MA Dissertation, University of Leicester.

Leetham, Sir A. (1918), 'Local War Museums', *Museums Journal*, 18,6:93–7.

Lewis, G. (1992a), 'Museums and their precursors: a brief world survey', and (1992b), 'Museums in Britain: a historical survey', in Thompson, J.M.A. (ed), *Manual of Curatorship: A Guide to Museum Practice*, (2nd ed), Oxford, Butterworth Heinemann.

McGuffie, T.H. (1964), *Rank and File: The Common Soldier at Peace and War 1642–1914*, London, Hutchinson and Co.

Moss, R.E.F. (1970), 'Regimental Museums', unpublished Museum Studies Dissertation, University of Leicester.

Museums and Galleries Commission (MGC), (1990), *The Museums of the Armed Services: Report of a Working Party 1990*, London, HMSO.

Newton, P. (1987a), 'Military museums and the Army Museums Ogilby Trust', *Museums Journal*, 87,2:67–9.

Newton, P. (1987b), 'The Ogilby Trusts', *The Bulletin of the Military Historical Society*, XXXV111, 148:148–50.

Oomen, D. (1992), 'A soldier's tale', *Museums Journal*, 92,4:49.

Pack, A.J. (1973), 'Portsmouth Royal Naval Museum', *Museums Journal*, 73,1:19–21.

Pearce, S.M. (1989), 'Museum studies in material culture: introduction', in Pearce, S.M. (ed), *Museum Studies in Material Culture*, London, Leicester University Press.

Pearce, S.M. (1990), 'Objects as meaning; or narrating the past', in Pearce, S.M. (ed), *New Research in Museum Studies; Volume 1, Objects as Knowledge*, Athlone.

Pearce, S.M. (1991), *Material Culture 2: Collection Studies*, unpublished notes for Museum Studies Course, University of Leicester, 1990–92.

Pereira, H.P.E. (1948), 'The Regimental Museum of the Worcestershire Regiment', *Museums Journal*, 48,3:55–6.

Pereira, H.P.E. (1950), 'Regimental Museums', *Museums Journal*, 49,7:235–7.

Preece, G. (1987), 'The Museum of the Manchesters: a social and regimental history', *Museums Journal*, 87,2:71–2.

Reid, W. (1971), 'The new National Army Museum', *Museums Journal*, 71,2:63–66.

Richards, D. (1991), in 'Soldiering on' by S. Wilkinson and I. Hughes, *Museums Journal*, 91,11:24.

Rivis, R.G.L. (1957), 'Local museums and the army', *Museums Journal*, 57,8:196–8.

Robertson, I. G. (1991), in 'Soldiering on' by S. Wilkinson and I. Hughes, *Museums Journal*, 91,11:26.

Sanger, E. (1993), *Englishmen at War: A Social History of Letters 1450–1900*, London, Alan Sutton.

Talbot Rice, E. (1984), 'News from the National Army Museum: museum education service', *The Bulletin of the Military Historical Society*, XXXV,137:14–15.

Taylor, E. (1993), 'What makes a subject sensitive?', *SHCG News*, 32, Summer 1993: 4–6.

Thomas, R. (1994), 'Fewer storms in the port', *Museums Journal*, 94,2:16.

Thorburn, W.A. (1962), 'Military history as a museum subject', *Museums Journal*, 62,3:187–93.

Thwaites, P.J. (1992), 'From Corps private collection to public museum: A history of the Royal Signals Museum 1920–1992', unpublished MA Dissertation, University of Leicester.

Tod, A. (1991), in 'Soldiering on', by S. Wilkinson and I. Hughes, *Museums Journal*, 91,11:25.

Turner, E.S. (1956), *Gallant Gentlemen: A Portrait of the British Officer 1600–1956*, London, Michael Joseph.

Warner, P. (1992), *The Great British Soldier: A Living History*, Newton Abbot, David and Charles.

Westrate, J.L. (1961), *European Military Museums: A Survey of Their Philosophy, Facilities, Programmes and Management*, Washington, Smithsonian Institution.

White, C. (1989), *The Royal Navy in Peace and War*, Andover, Pitkin Pictorials Ltd.

Wilkinson, P. (1993), 'Living history', in Fleming, D., Paine, C., and Rhodes, J.G., (eds), *Social History in Museums: A Handbook for Professionals*, London, HMSO.

Wilkinson, S. and I. Hughes, (1991), 'Soldiering on', *Museums Journal*, 91,11:23–8.

Wilson, Sir D. (1992), 'National museums', in Thompson, J.M.A., (ed), *Manual of Curatorship: A Guide to Museum Practice*, (2nd ed), Oxford. Butterworth Heinemann.

Wilson, G. (1993), 'Treachery and praise', *Museums Journal*, 93,9:32–4.

Wood, S. (1986a), '"Wha's like us?": a personal view of the way ahead for Scotland's military museums', *Museums Journal*, 86,1:13–15.

Wood, S. (1986b), 'Too serious a business to be left to military men: a personal view of the military museum's role today', *Museums*, 38,1:20–6.

Wood, S. (1987a), 'Obfuscation, irritation or obliteration?: The interpretation of military collections in British museums of the 1980s', *SHCG Journal*, 15, 1987–8: 4–6.

Wood, S. (1987b), 'Military museums: the national perspective', *Museums Journal*, 87,2:65–6.

Wood, S. (1990), 'Good news and bad news', *Journal of the Society for Army Historical Research*, LXVIII, 275:210.

Index